God bless

WAYS TO LIVE A SUCCESSFUL
Christian Life

Jasmine

WAYS TO LIVE A SUCCESSFUL
Christian Life

Ten dynamic ways to live a Successful Christian Life in The 21st century

JASMINE P. CHAMBERS

authorHOUSE®

AuthorHouse™
1663 Liberty Drive
Bloomington, IN 47403
www.authorhouse.com
Phone: 1-800-839-8640

Bible quotes are from the New International Version and unless otherwise stated

The New Kings James Version
The New Living Translation
New Bible Commentary
Strong Concordance

Published by AuthorHouse   10/30/2012

ISBN: 978-1-4670-0762-7 (sc)
ISBN: 978-1-4670-0763-4 (e)

TABLE OF CONTENTS

FOREWORD

Initially, I knew Jasmine Chambers as a church sister, then our relationship developed to that of close friends and now I know her in her new vocation as a writer. During a recent discussion with her, I discovered many dynamic things about her, which I will now share with you as you start your journey of reading this life-transforming book.

Jasmine was born and raised in Providence District, Lluidas Vale, St. Catherine, Jamaica. She was educated in Jamaica and brought up by her grandparents, who taught and nurtured her in the Lord. In her teenage years she gave her life to God. Her love, dedication and compassion for the Lord motivated her to serve in her local church and other neighbouring churches in various ministries, including women's ministry, teaching and hospitality. She loves people and wants to see them prosper in every area of their lives. Jasmine's testimony is to her grandparents, whom she loved very much and who were a great influence on her life.

When asked what inspired her to write this book, Jasmine replied that at a mid-week prayer meeting in her local church the Lord began to speak to her. She was not clear what the Lord was saying at the time, but a week later it became very clear when He visited her early one morning and told her, "I want you to write a book."

She found the experience so frightening and challenging that all she could do was to shout out these words: "No, Lord, you know I can't write a book! I struggled so much to find words to write when I was studying, so there is no way I can ever find enough to write a book. No, I can't do it."

Even though she loved reading, she did not believe she could write. But in spite of her complaints and doubts, the Lord did not change His Words. Later that night Jasmine listened to a CD by Matthew Ashimolowo which she had purchased two years earlier but had never got around to listening to. It was about the woman whose husband had died and who was in debt (2 Kings 4). She went to Elijah and he spoke to her, asking what was in her house and she replied that she had oil. Elijah instructed her to close the door and borrow vessels from her neighbours and start pouring the oil, then to sell what she had in her house and pay her debt.

The Lord then made it clear to Jasmine that all the resources she needed were in her house. For example, she had Bibles, books, a computer and commentaries—but the best resource was herself. An awesome anointing was released upon her that empowered her to start writing.

As we talked further, Jasmine revealed that, taking a step of faith, she took an A4 writing pad and started to write as the Holy Spirit directed her. Her first draft of ten chapters was written by hand within two weeks. Then, for the next few months, she was debating if she should put it on to the computer. Three months after the first handwritten draft, one of her church brothers came to her and shared that the Lord had told him to ask her when was she going to start writing her second book. It was at this stage that she finally decided to start typing her work on the computer.

Jasmine confirmed that the whole process of writing her book up to the time of writing the foreword took approximately two-and-a-half years.

When I asked if she had to face any particular challenges during this project, she told me that she had struggled to write the chapter about continuous learning. She asked the Lord to help her and the Lord spoke to her, saying that she needed to tell the readers, "Study about me!" This revelation is what assisted her to make her breakthrough in the writing.

I posed the question, 'What is your personal message to the reader?"
She replied that she hopes that they will read the contents of her
book and practise what is written, and as they do, their lives will be
transformed: they will be strengthened, empowered and experience
a successful Christian life.

My final question to Jasmine was, 'How would you like this book to
minister to the reader?' Jasmine said that she would love people to
read the book and realise that the key to their transformation only
starts when they apply the values and principles that are recorded
within each chapter. She referred to the chapter about prayer,
where she looks at Jesus's life of prayer and then advises the reader
how to pray.

In a nutshell, Jasmine's hope is that people will be blessed and inspired
to come to know Jesus and then be patient, trust in God and apply
the principles. This is how the book will transform their lives.

Ester Watson, B.A. (Hons)

DEDICATION AND ACKNOWLEDGEMENTS

I would like to thank the LORD, my mother and father, and my grandparents, Arthur and Hepsy Fuller. My uncle Glenroy and Clarice Lattery, Aunty Elaine Gordon and the rest of my precious family, with special thanks to my cousins, Orlean, Sonia and Ken, who have been of great support to me over the years. Pastor Calvin and Pauline Young, Pastor Sandra and Kevin Thomas and all my brothers and sisters at Mount Zion Community church in Aston.

Also Sharon Edwards, whose support during this project was invaluable, my dear friends Ester, Marcia and Veron for their assistance, and all my friends, near and far, present and past. I thank you from the bottom of my heart.

INTRODUCTION

It is the desire of all believers to live a successful Christian life.

To be successful equals being victorious in every area of our lives. Jesus clearly echoes this when he states, *I have come that they may have life and have it to the full* (John 10:10, NIV). There are certain principles from the Word of God that we all have to follow in order to live a victorious Christian life. Some of these principles will be outlined in this book.

The foundation of this book, *Ways To Live A Successful Christian Life*, stems from the Word of God. Here you can find instructions as God laid them out in His Word for you to follow. For example, God's Word tells us how we are to love Him with all our heart, soul, mind and strength, and to love each other, and be kind and forgiving. This book also instructs us how to receive His blessings, and take care of our spouse, rear our children and train them in the way they should go. It shows children how they should be obedient to their parents. The Word of God gives us answers to difficult questions, over which we may ponder. He reveals things to us as we read His Word.

However, this book cannot be classed as a substitute for God's Word. It is written with you in mind, to support your devotional pursuit of God's presence, His goodness and His favour and, as we read, this book should help us to obtain God's favour, to resist temptations and to be strong, focused Christians, overcoming every battle and adverse circumstances and serving God's purposes.

I pray as you read *How to Live a Successful Christian Life* with a sober mind God's Words will leap off the pages and penetrate your inner being to work the good successful works that God has called you to, and empowered you to do. I also pray that you will be imbued with power on High to know how rich and how great the love of GOD, in Christ Jesus towards you is as you put Him first and seek His will and purposes to achieve a successful life.

Chapter One

READ AND OBEY THE WORD OF GOD

One of the most important aspects in all believers' lives is to read, meditate, and obey the Word of God. The Word of God is given to strengthen, instruct and to build our faith in the Lord Jesus.

The Lord told Joshua that he was to read the Word and meditate on it day and night and in doing so he would prosper. It reads:

> Do not let this book of the law depart from your mouth; meditate on it day and night,so that you may be careful to do everything written in it. Then you will be prosperous and be successful.

> (Joshua 1:8)

The scripture also declared that we are to:

> Take to heart all the words I have solemnly declared unto you this day, so that you may command your children carefully all the words of this law.

> (Deut. 32:46)

These same principles still apply to us today. It is imperative that we take time to read, meditate, repeat and obey God's Word. His Word is a remarkable gift to humanity.

God's Word existed from the beginning of creation. The Bible tells us that:

In the beginning was the Word, and the Word was with God and the Word was God.

(St John 1:1 NIV)

As we read and study the scripture, we will discover many remarkable ways in which God used His Word. For example, God used His Word to create things, to give instruction, to guide and to bless. Our Lord used His Word to speak this massive world and all that is in it into existence. (See Genesis 1) By God's word were the heavens made and their starry host by the breath of his mouth (Psalms 33:6). God also spoke His Word and gave instruction to the first man, Adam, and told him to eat from all the trees in the garden, except from the tree of knowledge of good and evil (Genesis 2:15-17 NIV).

God also directed Abram with His Word to leave his country and his people and promised that he would bless him magnificently and make him great:

The Lord has said to Abram, 'Leave your country, your people and your father's household and go to the land I will show you. I will make you into a great nation and I will bless you; and I will make your name great, and you will be a blessing. I will bless those who bless you, and whoever curses you I will curse; and all people on earth will be blessed through you.

(Genesis 12:1-3)

He also spoke His Word to Moses and gave him the law to read to both adults and children.

When all Israel comes to appear before the Lord your God at the place he will choose, you shall read this law before them in their hearing. Assemble the people, men, women and children, and the aliens living in the towns, so they can listen and learn to fear the Lord your God and follow carefully all the words of his law.

(Deut. 31:11-12)

The Word of God is also evident in the New Testament. Jesus Himself is referred to as The Word (John 1:1).

He also used the Word on many occasions. Jesus used The Word to put the devil to shame. For example, when He was tempted by the devil after fasting for forty days, the devil asked him to turn stone into bread. But our Lord used the awesome Word and put the devil in his place, He let the devil know that: *Man does not live by bread alone but on every word that comes from the mouth of God (*Matthew 4:4).

Jesus spoke The Word to heal many who were sick (See Matt. 4:23) and taught many people The Word (Matthew 4:23-24). He took time to explain how important it was to put The Word into practice:

Therefore everyone who hears these words of mine and puts them into practice is like a wise man who builds his house on the rock. The rain came down, and the streams rose and the winds blew and beat against the house; yet it did not fall, because it had its foundation on the rock. But everyone who hears these words of mine and does not put them into practice is like a foolish man who builds his house on the sand. The rain came down, the streams rose, and the winds blew and beat against the house, and it fell with a great crash.

(Matthew 7:2-27)

He stated that The Word He had spoken is spirit and life (John 6:63). And He said that if we remain in Him and His Word remains in us, we can ask for whatever we wish and it will be given to us.

Remain in me, and I in you. No branch can bear fruit by itself; it must remain in the vine. Neither can you bear fruit unless you remain in me. I am the vine; you are the branches. If a man remains in me and me in him, he will bear much fruit; apart from me you can do nothing. If anyone doesn't remain in me he is like a branch that is thrown away and withers; such a branch is picked up, thrown in the fire and burnt. If you remain in me and my Words remain in you, ask whatever you wish and it will be given to you. This is my Father's glory that you bear much fruit showing yourself to be my disciples.

(John 15:4-8 NIV)

Jesus executed The Word in many forms while He was here on Earth and he has left many great examples for us follow.

There are many other great examples of believers who used God's Word and brought great transformation to people's lives. For example, Peter and John spoke the Word to the beggar (Acts 3:6) and transformed his life. The apostle Paul also preached and taught many people God's enduring Word in various places (Acts, 17, 18, 19).

God's Word is amazing and has been effective throughout all generations. Peter described the Word as living and enduring and must be craved for as new-born babies crave milk (1 Peter 2:1). The Psalmist tells us how important it is to hide His Word in our heart that we will not sin against Him (Psalm 119:11).

His Word is the foundation on which we stand and it is essential that we all take time to read it, meditate on it and obey it. His Word is available to all of us in its written form, **The Bible.**

- It is a unique book.
- It is available for public inspection.
- It is available to study.
- It is available to repeat.
- It is appropriate for all ages.
- It is able to inform us of the past, the present and future.
- It generates faith, life and hope.

- It tells us about Jesus.
- And it is good for discussion.

There are no limits to the extent of wisdom, teaching and understanding the Bible provides. It contains sixty-six books, including those of both the Old and New Testaments. The Bible was written by many authors. The first five books are known as the Pentateuch. It has different sections, some historical, some poetry and some are books of the prophets. The New Testament contains the Gospels, letters from the Apostle Paul and many other books, including the book of Revelation. The Bible is often referred to as our milk and bread; this splendid book contains spiritual food that will enable us to grow in Christ. There are numerous translations of the Bible and we can choose whichever translation suits us best.

To those among you who have never read a Bible before, and have not yet accepted the Lord Jesus as Saviour of your life, I would encourage you to purchase a Bible and start reading it. It will enlighten your understanding of our Lord Jesus. You will learn of His love, how He paid the highest price for us and wants us all to accept Him as Lord of our lives. You will also discover all the work He did while He was here on Earth and that He is coming back to judge and reward us. The Bible teaches us how to live our lives and be victorious, how to avoid temptation, to practise love, joy, kindness and goodness (Galatians 5:21-24).

To those of another faith, if you have never read the Bible, and if you want to read about Jesus and His great love, what it is to be born again and inherit eternal life, I would advise you, too, to purchase and read a Bible. As you read, you will learn and discover more truth about Jesus, the magnificent price He paid for humanity and His desire to see unity, peace and love reign in our heart. His Word is absolute truth (John 17:17). There is power, hope, wisdom and forgiveness in His Word, so please read this book!

For all New Believers, if you have just started reading the Bible, welcome to this pulsating book! Let the Word of Christ reside in you richly; there is so much to learn from it. With so many books and chapters in the Bible, maybe you are wondering which book to start with. It is important that you aim to read all the books. Nonetheless, as a new believer, you should begin with the books of the New Testaments, especially the book of John. But do not stop at this one book. There is something superb in all the other books; they can all help you to grow and build your confidence and faith in the Lord. We are to let the word of Christ dwell in us richly (Col. 3:16), so continue to read and allow His Word to fill your heart. The only way we can have His Word in us richly is by reading, researching, repeating, remembering and meditating on it continually. The Bible is able to aid us to:

- Teach and admonish one another (Col. 3:16).
- Correct and train others in righteousness (2 Tim. 3:16).
- Share instruction (Galatians 6:6).
- Assist us in giving thanks (1 Thessalonians 2:13).
- Encourage us (Hebrews 12:5).
- Enable us to preach to others (2 Timothy 4:2).

It is good for us to study His Word with others, with a friend or in a group. As we read and discuss it, it enables us to increase in knowledge and confidence. We are blessed whenever we read His Word (Psalms 1:2).

To those of you who have been reading and following the Bible's teaching, continue to reading, meditate and believe. You will never regret your time spent in God's Word. I am sure that you must have proven Him over and over in your life already. Do not give up on His Word and promises. Maybe you have not seen some of the promises come to pass as yet, but continue reading, speaking and believing His Word over every circumstance. His Word is still active, able to frighten the devil. Keep trusting and I am sure you will see His Word come to pass in due time. Remember that heaven and earth will pass away, but His Word will never pass away (Matt. 24:35). And as you continue to read and meditate you will always learn something new and refreshing from His Word; there are always new revelations coming to us from this inspiring book. Everything else can fail but

His Word never fails. *The grass withers and the flowers fall, but the word of the Lord stands for ever* (Isaiah 40:8).

If you have been discouraged or are feeling discouraged because of circumstances, start reading and believing again. Do not let the enemy rob you of this precious Word. The Word of God stated clearly that the enemy's intention is to destroy us. His plan is to steal, kill and destroy (John 10:10a). He wants to steal our confidence, our happiness, health, skills, abilities and future. If possible, give children a Bible from an early age and encourage them to read and study God's Word. We should make it our priority to introduce them to this breath-taking book even while they are very young. Remember that it is filled with truth!

There is no specific day, week, month or year assigned to us to read this book. You can read whenever it is convenient for you. However, it is highly recommended that a daily diet of God's Word can produce a healthy, fruitful life. I suggest that it is important to rise early in the morning and read His Word. God will always speak into our life and order our day as we rise and read His Word early in the morning. His Word will enable us to stand throughout the day and we are to declare it over all issues.

None of us will be able exhaust all that the Bible contains. Nonetheless, the following gives an A-Z outline of some of the awesome promises and blessings that it contains:

- **Abide**: *I am the vine, you are the branches. He who **abides** in me and me in him bears much fruit, for without me you can do nothing* (John 15:5).
- **Blessings**: *Then the land will yield its harvest, and God our God will **bless** us* (Psalm 67:6 NIV).
- **Comforter**: *The Lord will surely **comfort** Zion and will look with compassion on all her ruins* (Isaiah 51:3).
- **Deliverer**: *Then the Lord knows how to **deliver** the godly out of temptations and to reserve the unjust under punishment for the day of judgement* (2 Peter 2:9b NKJV).

- **Enlarge**: *Enlarge the place of your tent, do not hold back; lengthen your cords, strengthen your stakes* (Isaiah 54:2).
- **Forgive**: *But that you may know that the Son of Man has authority on earth to **forgive** sins* (Luke 5:24).
- **Giver**: *What, then, shall we say in response to this? If God is for us, who can be against us? He who did not spare His own Son, but gave Him up for us all, how will He not also, along with Him, graciously **give** us all things?* (Romans 8:31).
- **Hope**: *But as for me, I shall always have **hope**; I will praise you more and more* (Psalm 71:14).
- **Instruct**: *I will **instruct** you and teach you in the way you should go* (Psalm 32:8a).
- **Joy**: *You have made known to me the path of life; you fill me with **joy** in your presence* (Psalm 16:11a).
- **Kind**: *Be **kind** and compassionate to one another, forgiving each other, just as in Christ God forgave you* (Ephesians 4:32).
- **Love**: *This is the message you heard from the beginning: We should **love** one another (1 John 3:11).*
- **Mercy**: *I will have **mercy** on which I have mercy* (Romans 9:15 NIV).
- **Near**: *Come **near** to God and He will come near to you (James 4:8 NIV).*
- **Obey**: ***Obey** the Lord your God and follow His commands and decrees that I give you today (Deuteronomy 27:10 NIV).*
- **Peace**: *Peace I leave with you; my **peace** I give you. I do not give to you as the world gives* (John 14:27 NIV).
- **Quiet life**: *Make it your ambition to lead a **quiet life*** (1 Thessalonians 4:11 NIV).
- **Restore**: *He **restores** my soul. He guides me in paths of righteousness for his name's sake* (Psalm 23:3).
- **Strong**: *Finally, be **strong** in the Lord and in His mighty power* (Ephesians 6:10 NIV).
- **True**: *All your words are **true**; all your righteous laws are eternal (*Psalms 119:160).
- **United**: *Believers would be encouraged, **united** in love so that they may know the mystery of God, namely Christ* (Colossians 2:2).

- **Victory:** *But you give us **victory** over our enemies, and put our adversaries to shame* (Psalm 44:7 NIV).
- **Wisdom:** *For the Lord Gives **wisdom** and from his mouth come knowledge and understanding* (Proverbs 2:6 NIV).
- **Xerxes:** *The King had to listen to the Word from the Woman of God, who trusted in her God and had seen great result. King **Xerxes** had to carry out God's command even when it wasn't in his plan.* (See Esther 4-10)
- **Yoke:** *Take my **yoke** upon you and learn from me, for I am gentle and humble in heart, and you will find rest for our souls. For my yoke is easy and my burden is light* (Matthew 11:29-30).
- **Zeal:** *Never be lacking in **Zeal**, but keep your spiritual fervour, serving the Lord* (Romans 12:11).

The Bible contains everything and we should continue reading, repeating and studying it.

MY PERSONAL EXPERIENCES WITH GOD'S WORD

As a child, I was taught to read God's Word by my grandparents. They taught me to read and repeat the books of the Bible from Genesis to Revelation. It wasn't something that I relished as a child, but as I grew older I realised how awesome the Word of God was. I had to turn to His Word many times and read and speak it. I grew to appreciate and trust in God's amazing Word. I am glad that I was brought up to read God's Word. I have learnt to love His precious, powerful, life-changing Word. I have found comfort, direction, healing, peace and hope from reading His Word.

I have had many difficult experiences in life; some were painful, unexpected and almost unbearable. For example, when I was diagnosed with fibroids in my womb, it was a frightening experience. I was petrified and felt that my life had come to an abrupt end. I was about to lose my womb and I did not have any children. I love children dearly, I wasn't married, and was about to lose my womb. It was scary! The situation seemed unbearable. During that period I cried, complained and asked many questions about why I had to go through such a traumatic situation.

At the time many members of my family and friends encouraged me to have surgery, but I refused. I just could not understand why I was facing this. I was in pain and experiencing lots of discomfort and was also bleeding heavily. But despite all this, nothing would convince me to lose my womb. I did not listen to anyone; I went through all that suffering and discomfort for seven years, a difficult and stressful experience.

After some time, I turned to the Word of God and read and the Lord spoke to me through His Word. I can remember getting scriptures such as these:

> *The Lord your God is with you. He is mighty to save. He will take great delight in you. He will quiet you with His love* (Zephaniah. 3:17 NIV).

> *Never will I leave you; never will I forsake you* (Hebrews 13:5b NIV).

He reminded me of His healing power and what He had done for others with scriptures such as:

> *The people brought to Jesus all who had various kinds of sickness and, laying His hands on each one, He healed them* (Luke 4:40).

Those were some of the many scriptures the Lord gave to me during my struggles. I had to apply those scriptures to my life and believe that God would take care of me. Today I can say I have proven Him in my life! I later had surgery and although I have no children of my own, my mentality has changed. The fear, trepidation and dread that I had before has disappeared. My life today has not turned out to be as I anticipated. I have found healing in Him: emotional healing, physical healing and I have proven His Word to be powerful, alive and true. Before the surgery everything appeared hopeless, destitute and empty. Sometimes it did appear as if my mental state was not going to change; everything seemed dull and unbearable. But as I continued to read, meditate and trust in His Word and wait on Him, I began to experience changes in my life. His Word comforted me; it gave me hope, wisdom and understanding. And now I have peace. God's Word can change any situation that we may face in life. There is deliverance in His Word.

Now I can recommend the Word of God to anyone; for any situation you may be facing in your life, you can turn to His Word and read, believe and speak them to change your circumstances. It can transform your life and do for you what no one else can offer. His Word is REMARKABLE! Just as it worked for me, it can do the same for you as you read and obey it.

Another of my testimonies of God's faithfulness to His Word is related to the scar tissue from my surgery, which was very uncomfortable to touch. But one night, while I was ministering to the LORD, I asked GOD to heal my body. I prayed over it, repeated God's Word. *By His stripes, I am healed. He was wounded and bruised for me* (Isaiah 53:3). *Whatever I asked, believing it shall be done.* I repeated those Word over my stomach and prayed to God. I woke up one morning HEALED! All the pain and scar tissue around my stomach was gone. I am perfectly healed today, praise the Lord!

Often times, whenever we are faced with problems, we phone a friend and may spend hours talking about our troubles. Many times we are looking for answers from others that only the Lord can give. I want to encourage you to turn to God's Word: read it! His Word has all the answers.

I am not discouraging anyone from speaking to their friends; we all need each other. I do speak to and depend on many of my friends, sometimes to pray for me and with me; I also do the same for them. We all need each other. Nevertheless, we are to give the Lord priority in our lives, spend time in His Word, read it and have faith in it to take us through all our difficulties. Faith comes by us hearing the Word (Romans 10:17). He is able to speak to us through His Word.

He will never let us down or forsake us. He loves us so much and He has given us His Word to build and comfort us. All the answers that we need are in His Word. He is able to do exceedingly and abundantly above what we can ask or imagine. Trust in His Word and hold firmly to the Word of the Lord. (See 1 Corinthians 15:2).

If you are about to have surgery, or experiencing any form of illness, turn to God, turn to His Word. Maybe you are experiencing the same illness that I suffered, or it could be one of your family members or your friend who is sick. Read God's Word and depend on Him to heal you. You can also declare His Word over you, such as:

- By His stripes I am healed.
- He was wounded and bruised for me.
- He is able to heal all my diseases.
- Jesus spoke the word and healed all sickness.
- There is healing in the name of Jesus.

In His Word, there is hope and healing that no one else can give. Some of the scriptures that we can read and repeat for healing are:

- Matthew 8:16
- Acts 28 :8
- James 5 :14

God has comforted me with His Word with many other problems I have encountered in life. For example, I have experienced painful rejection in relationships, which made me cry for many months. I felt let down, dejected and acted like a loser. But the Lord stepped into the situation and comforted me with His Word. As I read the scriptures, He spoke to me and let me know that He loves and cares for me, and that I should not be troubled but trust in Him (John 14:1-2). God's Word healed my broken heart. He is always with us and willing to give us His Word to heal us.

Maybe you have been rejected by your husband, partner, family member, friends, or by your children. Maybe you are feeling unloved, insecure or broken at this moment. I want you to know that Jesus loves you, and He cares for you. He is more than able to comfort you with His Word. Please turn to God's Word and read it and repeat it. You can always find comfort and strength in His Word.

Jesus was also rejected by men. He came to earth to do good, to heal, save, bless and restore humanity, yet He was rejected. Most of us will experience some form of rejection in this life. So if you are experiencing this, don't be dismayed. You can turn your rejection into direction by reading His Word and applying it to your situation. Listen to what He is saying to you. It is also necessary to develop a positive attitude as you read.

Rejection can prevent you from fulfilling your dreams, vision and maximising your potential. But speak God's positive Word over your life. Speak these Words if you have been rejected:

- I am an over-comer.
- I am blessed and created to rule.
- I am more than a conqueror.
- He has given me power and authority over all fear.
- I am a child of a king.
- If Jesus is with me, who can be against me?
- I am above and not beneath.
- I have got Jesus on my side.

I have also found hope in His Word when I was experiencing financial difficulties. When I came to England from Jamaica, it was a difficult phase, a time of stress and strains; financially I was low. I had to rely on family and friends for financial assistance, which was embarrassing. I was confused, depressed and unhappy. Sometimes I wasn't working and I struggled to find food, clothes or to purchase anything. But I prayed during those times, and read His Word and trusted in Him. Many times I was given scriptures that gave me hope and spoke about the situation I was in, such as this:

> *Therefore, I tell you, do not worry about your life, what you will eat or drink; or about your body, what you will wear.*

Is not your life more important than food, and the body more important than clothes?

Look at the birds of the air; they do not sow or reap or store away in barns, and yet your heavenly Father feeds them. Are you not more valuable than they? Who of you by worrying can add a single hour to his life? And why do you worry about clothes? See how the lilies of the field grow. They do not labour or spin. Yet I tell you that not even Solomon in all his splendour was not dressed like one of these (Matthew 6:25-29 NIV).

You won't be disappointed in filling your life with His pulsating Word. Have faith in His Word and let the Lord turn all the impossible circumstances into workable situations. If you are experiencing financial struggle at this time, please confess these blessings over your life:

- I am blessed in the city.
- I am blessed in the field.
- I am blessed in daily provision.
- I am blessed financially.
- From this day on God will bless me.

The following are some of the scriptures I have learnt over the years. I have repeated them over my life, over and over. You can do the same or choose some of your own and repeat them. It worked for me and it can work for you, too.

- *Therefore, there is now no condemnation for those who are in Christ Jesus, who do not live according to the sinful nature but according to the Spirit* (Romans 8:1NIV).
- *For God so loved the world that He gave His only begotten Son, that whoever believes in him shall not perish but have eternal life. For God did not send His Son into the world to condemn the world, but to save the world, through Him* (John 3:16-17 NIV).
- *What, then, shall we say in response to this? If God is for us, who can be against us?* (Romans 8:31).

- *The Lord is my shepherd, I shall not want. He makes me to lie down in green pastures, he leads me beside quiet waters, and He restores my soul. He guides me in path of righteousness for his name's sake. Even though I walk through the valley of the shadow of death. I will fear no evil, for you are with me; your rod and your staff they comfort me. You prepare a table before me in the presence of my enemies. You anoint my head with oil; my cup overflows. Surely goodness and love will follow me all the days of my life, and I will dwell in the house of the Lord for ever (Psalm 23 1-6 NIV).*
- *No weapon forged against you will prevail and you will refute every tongue that accuses you. This is the heritage of the servants of the Lord, and this is their vindication from me declares the Lord (Isaiah 54:16-17).*

His Word can create positive alteration in our lives.

DISOBEDIENCE

There are severe consequences whenever we disobey God's Word. Disobedience can delay our blessings and even prevent them. We are blessed when we hear the Word of God and obey it (Luke 11:28). We should strive to be obedient to God's Word. I can remember going into a relationship that the Lord had warned me against and I had to pay the consequences for my action. We should listen and do what He tells us to do, in His Word. I can remember getting scriptures during my time telling me to wait on the Lord, and be of good courage.

> *Do not be yoked together with unbelievers. For what do righteousness and wickedness have in common? Or what fellowship can light have with darkness? What harmony between Christ and Belial? What does a believer have in common with an unbeliever? (1 Corinthians 14-15 NIV).*

I did not listen to the Lord and went into the relationship at my own choosing and ended up embarrassed, let down and rejected and had to pick my life up and start afresh. We are to obey Him whenever He speaks to us.

Some years ago, one of my friends went into a marriage that the Lord had warned her against. She disobeyed and went into the marriage. It wasn't long after that she was beaten, cheated on, robbed and insulted, in front of others. The Word of God says there are consequences for our disobedience (Ephesians 5:6).

We also read in the scripture of people who suffered because they disobeyed God's word. There was a prophet whom the Lord sent out and instructed him not to stop at anyone's home, but he disobeyed the Lord's Word and was later eaten by a lion. (See 1 Kings 13). Jonah also disobeyed the Lord and ended up in the belly of a fish. Whenever we disobey God's Word there are always unpleasant consequences. Let's strive to be obedient to His Word.

THE RELEVANCE OF THE WORD IN THE TWENTY-FIRST CENTURY

It is still important to read, repeat and obey His Word in this 21st century. His Word is fitting for all generations. The scripture states that Our Lord does not take back His Word from us (Isaiah 31:2). None of us should be starved to death from spiritual malnutrition in our generation. We are to take time and read His Word. God's Word is still our strong foundation. It is still active and alive for us to apply in our generation. The scripture tells that if anyone obeys His Word, God's love is made complete in him (1 John 2:5).

We are to obey His Word and put it into practice in our generation.

- We are to purchase Bibles and read them.
- We are to ask the Lord for things based on His Word.
- We are to speak His word in prayer.
- We are to teach His Word to our children.
- We are to use it for teaching, rebuking, correcting and training (1 Timothy 3:16).
- We are to apply His Word to all situations.
- We are to preach His Word.
- We are to love His Word.
- We are to abide in His Word.

- His Word still remains powerful.
- And we are to obey His Word.

His Word is still relevant today. The apostle Paul said, by the gospel we are saved, and that we are to hold firmly to the word preached to us. Peter said it is for ever (Peter 1:23-25). Moses wrote the law and read it to all the men, women and children. Those children who did not know the law heard it and learned to fear the Lord (Deut 31:12-13). It is still crucial for us to do all these things with His Word, to teach it to our children, and to depend on His Word to direct us. We need His Word to function properly. The Bible says that the men and women in the past were not different from us and they trusted in His Word and experienced great miracles. We can do the same. Elijah was a man just like us (James 5:17). Elijah was able to go and speak God's Word to Ahab, the king of Israel who committed murder and wanted to take over Naboth's possessions, but the Lord revealed His Word to Elijah and told him to go and speak to the king and to warn him of his action. Elijah went and did what the Lord told him and his word brought conviction (1 Kings 21:17-20).

The people in biblical times depended on the Word, they spoke it, had faith in it and it worked for them. It still has the same power today if we put it to work. Paul said that he had to give thanks for the Thessalonian believers, because they accepted God's Word and it worked in their lives (see Theses. 2:13-14). God's Word is still able to work for us today and we are to speak it to give life in our world today. We are to learn how to handle God's Word properly and to use it appropriately in this generation.

Our world is filled with all kinds of heart-wrenching situations. But we are to read His Word and confess it over these issues. We are seeing and hearing of distressing situations daily. We are experiencing crime, child abduction and murder of our children, stabbing, fighting, unemployment, war, divorce, violence, killing in our own neighbourhoods. The world we live in is filled with all kinds of evil. We all need to speak the powerful Word of God over these matters.

In the UK in 2009, it was reported by Crimestoppers UK that 60 per cent of rescued trafficked children later go missing from authority care. (Crimestoppersuk.org 2010)

We are also experiencing all kinds of immoral activities: prostitution, fornication, adultery, lying, stealing, involvement in witchcraft, disobedience, backbiting and many other ungodly activities.

According to recent research, shoplifting has increased sharply during the recession and 22,000 shop staff suffered violence in the UK in 2010. Furthermore, a report from the Youth Justice Board in March 2009 states that one in three youths carries a knife or gun and a crime is committed by a young person every two minutes.

Reading and hearing about all these depressing conditions in our world is frightening. But the Word is here for us to teach our young people and to speak over these problems. God's Word is spirit and life (John 6:63) and it is enduring. Peter told us that it stands forever: *For you have been born again, not of perishable seeds but of imperishable, through the living and enduring word of God. For all men are like grass, and all their glory is like the flowers of the field; the grass withers and the flowers fall, but the Word of the Lord stands forever* (1 Peter 1:23-25).

We are to read His Word and speak them over these issues. We can only get His Word inside of us by reading it, not by listening to others, or by placing the Bible in our bags, or on our shelves, but by taking time to read it ourselves. There is a Word in the Bible for every issue that we may face. His Word is living and is able to penetrate every situation. Let us look at a very frightening situation that confronted the disciples and Jesus. He was able to speak to it and calm the storm. The Bible says that:

> *One day Jesus said to his disciples, let's go over to the other side of the lake, so they got into a boat and set out. As they sailed, he fell asleep. A squall came down on the lake, so that the boat was being swamped and they were in great danger. The disciples went and woke him, saying, 'Master, Master, we*

are going to drown!' He got up and rebuked the wind and the raging waters. The storm subsided, and all was calm.

(Luke 8:22-25)

Jesus spoke to frightening situations and was able to change circumstances with His Word.

The following are some scriptures that we can read and speak for some of the situations we may encounter in life.

- Attack. Psalm 35:1, 2, Luke 23:34.
- Bereavement. Psalm:147:3, 1 Thessalonians 4:13-18.
- Divorce. Mark10:1-12, Romans 7:2, 3.
- Drug abuse. Proverbs 1:10, 2 Peter 2:19.
- Danger. Psalm 12:1, 1 Peter 13, 14.
- Sexual immorality. Proverbs 5 1-12.
- Sickness. Matthew 25:36.
- Marriage. Mark 10:1-12, Ephesians 5:21-33.
- Failure. Psalm 73:26, Hebrews 4:14-16.
- Intimidation. Psalm 3:1-3.
- Insults. 69:9.
- Pain. 103:1-4.

If we refuse to fill our heart with the Word of God, there are many other unpleasant situations that can quickly creep in and take up residence in our hearts. Mark mentioned many of these, such as hopelessness, evil thoughts, sexual immorality, theft, murder, adultery, greed, malice, deceit, envy, slander, arrogance and madness (Mark 7:21). These evils can dominate our lives if we constantly refuse to read His Word. But they can all be avoided if we feed on His powerful Word. The Psalmist declared that if God's Word is hidden in our hearts, it will prevent us from sinning. (See Psalms 119:11) His Word is able to pull down the enemy's plan and give us deliverance. All we need to do is to take the helmet of salvation and the sword of the Spirit, which is the Word of God (Ephesians 6:17) and allow His Word to dwell richly in us (Gal. 3:16).

Many believers, evangelists, preachers, pastors are applying His Word today all over the world, and are seeing all kinds of situations disappearing: sickness and diseases cured, the lives of drug addicts and offenders transformed, marriages restored and many are accepting the Lord Jesus. The Word of God is still relevant for us to today and it will enable us to lead a successful Christian life as we continue to read, repeat, and believe it. His Word is living and enduring (1 Peter 1:23).

His Word is also sweeter than honey to our lips (Psalm 119:103). So let us speak positive words in our generation and change our circumstances:

- I am the righteousness of God.
- I am blessed.
- I am highly favoured.
- I am a child of the king.
- I will put God's Word into practice.
- I do not live on bread alone but on the Word of God.
- His Word is my strong foundation.
- God is able to put me in charge of many things.
- I will pour out my worship to the Lord.
- I am fearfully and wonderfully made.
- I am justified by faith.
- I am complete in Christ.
- I am blessed spiritually.
- I am blessed emotionally.
- I am blessed financially.
- I have power to gain wealth.
- I will make Jesus known to the world.
- I will serve my purposes in my generation.
- God's spirit will guide me all the way.
- In Him I have peace.
- From this day on, He will bless me.

The Lord is also speaking to us through His Word in our generation to serve Him. It is crucial that we take time and listen to His Word when it is preached to us and be obedient and come and have fellowship with Him. His Word stated: *Behold I am coming soon! Blessed is he who keeps the word of the prophet in this book* (Revelation 22:7). God is saying to all of us in this generation to come and have a relationship with Him, He is speaking to children, women, fathers, and young men (1 John 12-14). And as we hear His Word, we are to yield to Him, because He loves us and wants us all to come and know Him as Lord.

This chapter has addressed the importance of reading the Word of God. It shows how God's Word worked from the beginning of creation. I have also outlined my own experiences with His Word and how important it is for us to obey it, read it, meditate, repeat and teach it. It also shows that none of us will remain stagnant as we continue to feed upon God's Word. It also mentions that God's Word is still relevant for the twenty-first century, and that Jesus is The Word. So let's continue to read, repeat, research, remember, obey and meditate on His life-changing Word. Jesus said, *Heaven and earth will pass away, but my words will never pass away.* (Luke 21:33). God's Word to Joshua is still applicable to us today.

> *Do not let this book of the Law depart from your mouth; meditate on it day and night, so that you may be careful to do everything written in it. Then you will be prosperous and be successful* (Joshua 1:8).

WHO CAN LIVE WITHOUT HIS WORD?

Chapter Two

THE SIGNIFICANCE OF PRAYER AND FASTING

Prayer together with fasting is one of the most important building blocks in all believers' lives. It is the main avenue that we use to communicate with our Lord. Therefore, it is crucial that we take time out to fast and pray. Prayer can do some of the most amazing works in our lives. For example, it:

- Brings us into deep fellowship with Christ.
- God will give us answers to our prayers.
- Prayer helps us to participate in the expansion of God's kingdom.
- And it also enables us to be strong and fruitful on our journey with God.

The scripture tells us that believers in both the Old and New testaments prayed sincerely. They prayed and the Lord heard and answered their prayers. Many have seen magnificent things happen in their lives. Some of those brave people were Solomon, Daniel, Isaac, Samson and Hanna.

The book of Chronicles tells how Solomon prayed and gave thanks and praises to the Lord. The Bible says that he spread out his hands towards heaven and made his request to God, both for himself and the people of Israel and the Lord heard him. (See 2 Chord. 6:1-22)

Daniel was also a great man of prayer. He prayed over many issues in his life and his prayer even saved him from lions. (See Daniel 6:8-10) Daniel's relationship with the LORD in prayer helped to strengthen and protect him from dangers and even when he faced a death threat he did not give up, he continued to pray to the Lord and he experienced a marvellous deliverance. (See Daniel 6)

This is one of Daniel's outstanding prayers.

> *O Lord, the great and awesome God, who keeps his covenant of love with all who love him and obey His commands, we have sinned and done wrong. We have been wicked and rebelled; we have turned away from your commands and laws.*
>
> *We have not listened to your servants the prophets, who spoke in your name to our kings, our princes and our fathers, and to all the people of the land.*
>
> *Lord, you are righteous, but this day we are covered with shame, the men of Judah and people of Jerusalem and all Israel, both near and far in all the countries where you have scattered us because of our unfaithfulness to you. O Lord, we and our kings, our princes and our fathers, are covered with shame because we have sinned against you.*
>
> *The Lord our God is merciful and forgiving, even though we have rebelled against him; we have not obeyed the Lord our God or kept the laws he gave us through his servants the prophets.*

(Daniel 9:4-11 NIV)

Isaac was another great man of prayer. He prayed to the Lord on behalf of his wife. He asked the Lord for a child when she was childless and the Lord heard him and answered his prayer and gave him the desire of his heart. The scripture says that later his wife Rebecca became pregnant and gave birth to twin boys, Esau and Jacob (Genesis 25:21-24).

Samson and **Hannah** also prayed to the Lord when they experienced difficult circumstances and the Lord heard their cries and delivered them.

Samson prayed and asked the Lord to remember him and to help him to regain his strength, so that he could revenge the Philistines who dug out his eyes. The Lord answered, his prayer and Samson regained his strength and was able to destroy all his enemies.

> *Then Samson prayed to the Lord, O Sovereign Lord, remember me. O Lord, please strengthen me just once more and let me with just one blow get revenge on the Philistines for my two eyes.*
>
> *Then Samson reached toward the two central pillars on which the temple stood. Bracing himself against them, his right hand on the one and his left hand on the other, Samson said, "Let me die with the Philistines!" Then he pushed with all his might, and down came the temple on the rulers and all the people in it. Thus he killed many more when he died than while he lived.*

(Judges 16:28-30)

Hannah: We read, too, about Hannah, how she cried out to the Lord in distress when she was childless. The scripture says she was ridiculed by people and she felt ashamed by her circumstance. But she cried out to the Lord in prayer and asked the Lord to give her a son. And our great God heard her and answered her prayer and gave her a son. (See 1 Samuel 1:10-20)

God is always hearing and answering His children's cries. Jesus our Saviour led a life of prayer while He was here on Earth. He prayed in many circumstances. He prayed at different times, He prayed publicly and privately. (See Mark 1:35 NIV) And He prayed for Himself, for His disciples and for us (John 17:1-26).

Jesus also left a pattern for us to follow. (See Matthew 6:9-14) The scripture tells that Jesus prayed with passion. It says: *And being in anguish, he prayed more earnestly and His sweat was like drops of blood falling to the ground* (Luke 22:44 NIV)

Jesus also encouraged us to pray earnestly, He says, we are to:

> *Ask and it will be given to you: seek and you will find; knock and the door will be open to you. For everyone who ask receives; he who seeks finds and to him who knocks, the door will be opened. Which of you, if his son ask for bread, will give him a scorpion? Or if he asks for a fish, will give him a snake? If you, then, though you are evil, know how to give good gifts to your children, how much more your Father in heaven gives good gifts to those who ask him.*
>
> (Matthew 7:7-11 NIV)

Jesus' disciples followed in His footsteps and devoted themselves to prayer (Acts 2:42). They were described as men of prayer. (Acts 9:40, 16:25, 28:8). The Book of Acts states that the church was born in the surroundings of prayer (Acts 1:14).

Paul and Silas prayed in prison until the earth was shaken. These men were placed in prison for preaching about Jesus in a threatening situation, surrounded with fear and uncertainties. But they did not give up because of their circumstance. They prayed, they cried out to the Lord at midnight and the Lord answered by sending an earthquake and shaking the prison where they were held (Acts 16:25-26 NIV).

Prayer is still effective in our world today. Jesus will never turn His back on us whenever we cry out to Him. The apostle Paul was convinced that the Lord would deliver him, so he wrote to the Philippians to let them know that he would be delivered.

> *For I know through your prayers and the help given by the Spirit of Jesus Christ, what has happen to me will turn out for my deliverance.*

(Philippians 1:19 NIV)

Jesus loves us so much that He gave his life for us. So nothing is too good for Him to give us whenever we ask in prayer. *Greater love has no man than this, that he lay down his life for his friends* (John 15:13 NIV).

The Psalmist states: *The Lord bestows favour and honour; no good thing does he withhold from those whose walk is blameless* (Psalm 84:11b)

As believers prayed in the past and trusted in the Lord to deliver them from various troubles, Our Lord Jesus is still expecting us to call upon His name. Jesus our Saviour prayed. As a result, it is crucial that we take time out to pray and seek Him in all circumstances. He will hear and answer us whenever we call.

> *This is the confidence we have in approaching God; that if we ask anything according to His will he hears us.*

(1 John 5:14)

We are encouraged not to be anxious about anything, but to go to Him with everything in prayer (Philippians 4:6). The scripture tells us that we are to devote ourselves to prayer.

> *For the eyes of the Lord are on the righteous and his ears are attentive to their prayers, but the face of the Lord is against those who do evil.*

(1 Peter 3:12 NIV)

If you are asking the question, how do I pray and what do I pray about? You are not on your own. Believers have asked this question over and over, especially new believers. And to be honest with you, it is **not** always easy to pray. But we can all learn to pray. None of us should feel afraid to speak to our Lord and we can speak to Him at any time, in our own words and in our own languages, and we can do it freely. God knows and understands all the words that we use. He knows all about us, even our thoughts.

May the Words of my mouth and the thought of my heart be pleasing to you, O Lord my rock and my redeemer.

(Psalms 19:14)

As we serve the Lord and continue to read His Word, have fellowship with Him, listen to the prayers of other believers, continue to love and serve Him, we will develop in confidence and be able to pray more fluently.

Our Lord Jesus will not condemn us or put us down because of our language, spiritual status or failures. Neither should we try to impress Him with long words. God is only impressed when we cry out to Him with a clean and pure heart. He wants us to pour out our hearts to Him. The effective, fervent prayer of a righteous man avails much (James 5:16).

Many of the great works carried out, were done by believers who were not eloquent speakers but they poured out their hearts to Lord, and He heard and answered their cries.

If you are still contemplating on how to speak to the Lord, you can use the following pattern, as you approach Him in prayer:

- Give Him thanks and praises.
- Ask Him to forgive you.
- Ask Him to help you to forgive others.
- Ask Him to supply your needs.
- Ask Him to bless and supply the needs of others.

It is important that we give thanks and praises as we seek the Lord in prayer. It is a very important element of prayer. The Philippians were encouraged to make supplication with thanksgiving in prayer as they made their petition to the Lord (4:6). The scripture also tells us that we are to be steadfast in prayer and to be watchful and thankful

(Colossians 4:2) and we are to: *Enter His gates with thanksgiving and His courts with praises* (Psalm 100:4).

He has done so much for us, we can all give Him thanks from our heart, so let us thank Him for:

- Sending Jesus, his only Son, to die for us.
- Thank him for saving you.
- Thank Him for His great provision.
- Thank Him for answering our prayers.
- Thank Him for our jobs.
- Thank Him for the roof over our heads.
- Thank Him for life.
- Thank Him for our families.
- Thank Him for each other.

Give Him thanks for all things. For the sunshine, the autumn, winter, spring, summertime and rain. Let us give the Lord thanks for all circumstances and event that He has allowed us to face in life. And let us also thank Him for His great love, compassion, favour, presence, greatness, forgiveness and for all His blessings, great and small.

Give thanks in all circumstances, for this is God's will for you in Christ Jesus.

(1 Thess. 5:18)

Praise: We should take time out to give Him praise He is worthy to be praised.

Among the gods there is none like you, O Lord; no deeds can compare like yours. All the nations you have made will come and worship before you, O Lord; they will bring glory to your name.

(Psalm 86:8-9 NIV)

Jesus' prayer begins with an element of praise. *Hallowed be thy name* (Matthew 6:9).

As we pray, we are to give Him praises and adore His name. There are many, many awesome words to use to tell Him how good and great and lovely He is. Tell Him that He is wonderful, He is great, He is mighty; He is adorable, He is holy and amazing. There is no god as remarkable as He is and He is the Saviour of the world.

The Psalmist tells us that we should honour Him and praise His holy name:

> *Praise the Lord, all you nations: extol him, all you peoples. For great is his love towards us, and the faithfulness of the Lord endures for ever* (Psalm:117).

We can shout His praises over all the Earth, in His house, at home, wherever it is convenient. We are to shout His praises because He is worthy of our praises and He also loves our praises.

> *My mouth will speak in praise of the Lord. Let every creature praise his holy name for ever and ever.*
>
> (Psalms 145:21 NIV)

We can also praise Him with instruments and at different places:

> *Praise God in his sanctuary; praise him in his mighty heavens. Praise him for his acts of power. Praise him for his surpassing greatness. Praise him with the sounding of the trumpet, praise him with the harp and lyre, praise him with tambourine and dance, praise him with the strings and flute, praise him with the claps of cymbals, praise him with resounding cymbals. Let everything that has breath praise the Lord.*
>
> (Psalms 150:1-6 NIV)

Ask Him for forgiveness: As we approach our Lord in prayer it is also necessary for us to ask the Lord to forgive us, so that we will be able to approach Him with cleans hands and pure heart. It is also important that we ask Him to help us to forgive others. It is stated plainly in His Word how essential it is for us to forgive others:

> *For if you forgive men when they sin against you, your heavenly Father will also forgive you. But if you do not forgive men their sins, your heavenly Father WILL NOT forgive your sins.*

> (Matthew 6:14-15 NIV)

Although none of us should always bring up our past sins to God, or always feel guilty of our past sins. The Lord has already forgiven us for our past sins. But there are times when we will fall short and lapse back into certain sins. We are to recognise them and confess them, and believe that He has forgiven us. Many times people who we trust and love will hurt us and sometimes we find it difficult to forgive. But the Word of God says we are to do away with all our sins:

> *Get rid of all bitterness, rage and anger, brawling and slander, along with every form of malice. Be kind and compassionate to one another, forgiving each other, just as in Christ God forgave you.*

> (Ephesians 4:31-32 NIV)

Make petition to Him: There are many needs and situations in life for us to take to the Lord in prayer. We are encouraged to take everything to Him in prayer. Nevertheless, we are to make an effort to pray for ourselves, our families, for our communities, for unbelievers, for our government, against sickness and diseases, for other brothers and sisters and for our nations.

Ourselves: As we approach the Lord in prayer we are to ask Him for:

- direction, protection, provision over our lives
- wisdom and favour

- cleansing through the blood of Jesus
- ask Him to strengthen us spiritually
- to help us to focus on Him, to give Him priority and serve Him with a clean and pure heart
- for wisdom, skills and understanding to be able to share the Good News to others well
- to help us to be obedient to His Word and to be courageous
- We should also ask Him to help us to be loving, kind and compassionate to others.
- Ask Him to help us to be able to discover our skills and potential, so that we will use them fully to serve His purposes.
- Ask Him for a heart of gratitude, praise, thanksgiving and worship.

Let us also remind ourselves of who we are and declare His Word over our lives daily, that we are:

- Redeemed by the blood of the Lamb.
- Complete in Him.
- Highly blessed and favoured.
- The righteousness of God.
- Over-comers
- Protected by angels.
- Members of the chosen generation.

As we pray we are to practise speaking positive words over our lives and to declare them as often as we can. God is able to do for us much more than we are able to ask and it is significant that we ask Him.

No eye has seen, no ear has heard, no mind has conceived what God has prepared for those who love him (1 Corinthians 2:9)

Families: Many families are messed up. There are so much pain, hurt and disappointment in families. We are to pray for our families. Some parents are killing their own children. While writing this book (in 2010) I heard of two parents who killed their children. Two were stabbed to death in England. I have also read of many children who have been abused physically, emotionally and sexually by their own families. We are to pray for our families in these difficult times. Let us ask God to:

- Save those who do not know Him.
- Let us ask for protection and favour on their lives.
- For peace and love to flow in their hearts.
- To heal brokenness and pain.
- For family members to be kind to each other.
- For families to show love and respect for others.
- To live exemplary lives.

God is able to break all the plans of the enemy and we have this brilliant privilege to take everything to Him in prayer. Jesus is our awesome Saviour who is able to do all that we ask. *The prayer of a righteous man is powerful and effective* (James 5:16b).

Our communities: As we pray for ourselves and our families, we are to take time out to pray for others in our communities.

- Ask the Lord to supply the needs of others in our communities.
- For His protection and provision for those in our communities.
- Ask Him to save souls, to forgive and to keep them in perfect peace.
- And forge unity and peace amongst us.

The Lord is always there at our side, caring, comforting, encouraging and guiding us. He will not reject our prayers. His Word declares: *Praise is to God who has not rejected my prayer or withheld His love from me!* (Psalms 66:20 NIV).

We are to pray against evils which destroy lives. The Lord Jesus has given us the authority to destroy these. We have the authority to bind and loose, to destroy all the plans of the enemy. The scripture says: *I have given you authority to trample on snakes and scorpions and to overcome all the powers of the enemy; nothing will harm you* (Luke 10:19 NIV).

Many communities are surrounded by dangerous gangs. We are to ask the Lord to save gang members, ask Him to break up these gangs and to give them a revelation of His love. Many of our young people have lost their lives because of gang association, and many are fighting against each other. Jesus is our source and we are to call upon His name and ask Him to save our communities. Pray against the enemy's plans, that they be destroyed in the name of Jesus. We are to pray as Paul told the Ephesians: *Pray in the Spirit on all occasions with all kinds of prayers and requests. With this in mind, be alert and always keep on praying for all the saints* (Ephesians 6:18 NIV).

Let us also pray against prostitution and violence in our community. Many of us have neighbours and family members who have lost their children in gang warfare; some are in prison or in hospital suffering from stab-wounds and gun-shot. But Our Lord is able to do all things. He is able to protect, to transform lives, to give hope and to change dark circumstances. *If we cry out to Him our prayers are powerful and effective to change any situation* (James 5:16).

We should also take time out to pray for our schools, teachers and students. Let us ask the Lord to help our young people to be kind to each other, to love each other, to respect each other, to be tolerant with each other. We are to ask for His protection and favour on their lives, to save those who do not know Him, to strengthen and keep them, to give them wisdom, to increase their knowledge and that they will learn and develop all their skills and talents.

We should also ask Him to strengthen our teachers, to protect them, that they will remain healthy and that they be kind, be patient and always give their best.

Unbelievers: There are many unbelievers in our world and many are around us. We are to pray for them.

- Ask the Lord to save them.
- Pray for courage, compassion and boldness to share the Good News to unbelievers.
- We are to pray for every race, tribe, class and sex.

- Ask Him to break the stubborn heart of stone.
- Ask Him to help us to be able to witness to others well.
- Ask Him for the bravery to speak to unbelievers.
- Pray that their ears, eyes and heart will be receptive to Jesus.
- For more workers
- Pray for missionaries.
- Pray against the fear of man which the devil uses to try and stop us from spreading the gospel.
- And always pray silently for all those you come across daily.

Other believers: Believers have always prayed for other believers. The scripture shows us many times that believers prayed for each other and even the strongest and the best Christians need to be prayed for. The apostle Paul told the Ephesians that they should keep on praying for all the saints (see Ephesians 6:18). There are so many other believers all over the world and it is essential that we pray for them and ask the Lord for His protection and favour on their lives. Look at this wonderful prayer Paul prayed for the Ephesian brethren:

> *For this reason I kneel before the Father, from whom His whole family in heaven and earth derives its name. I pray that out of His glorious riches He may strengthen you with power through His Spirit in your inner being, so that Christ may dwell in your hearts through faith. And I pray that you, being rooted and established in love, may have power together with all the saints, to grasp how wide and long and high and deep is the love of Christ and to know this love that surpasses knowledge, that you may be filled to the measure of all the fullness of God.*

(Ephesians 3:14-19 NIV)

The above prayer is an ideal prayer for other brothers and sisters.

The Psalmist declares: *Know that the Lord has set apart the godly for himself; the Lord will hear when we call on him* (Psalm 4:3 NIV)

There are missionaries, pastors, evangelists, teachers and other believers on mission all over the world, some in dangerous places. Paul also asked the Thessalonians to pray for the missionaries:

Finally, brothers, pray for us that the message of the Lord may spread rapidly and be honoured, just as it was with you. And pray that we may be delivered from wicked and evil men, for not everyone has faith. But the Lord is faithful and He will strengthen and protect you from the evil one.

(Theses 3:1-3)

And pray for us, too, that God may open a door for our message, so that we may proclaim the mystery of Christ, for which I am in chains. Pray that I may proclaim it clearly, as I should be.

(Colossians 4:2-4 NIV)

Continue to pray for believers and ask the Lord that they will:

- have patience and endurance
- honour and please the Lord
- know the Lord better and be strengthened in Him
- gain spiritual wisdom
- And to stay in Christ joy and continue to give Him thanks and praises

Sickness: There are all kinds of stubborn sicknesses and diseases in many of our bodies and we are to pray against them. Sickness and disease can be disappeared as we pray and ask in the powerful resurrected name of JESUS. So let us command all sicknesses to go! Cancer, backache, headache and all pains to leave our bodies in the name of Jesus. Let us also take authority over suicidal tendency, depression, brokenness and fear. All bondages, captivities, and oppressions are loosed in the name of Jesus. Jesus came to set us free and we are free.

Continue to speak the word of healing over your life. If you are sick, His Word says: *That we are healed by his stripe and Jesus took up our infirmities and carried our diseases* (Matthew 8:17).

James also mentioned that we should pray. We are to pray in faith if we are troubled or sick.

> *Is any one of you in trouble? He should pray. Is anyone happy? Let him sing songs of praise. Is any one of you sick? He should call the elders of the church to pray over him and anoint him with oil in the name of the Lord. And the prayer offered in faith will make the sick person well; the Lord will raise him up. If he has sin he will be forgiven. Therefore confess your sins to each other and pray for each other so that you may be healed. The prayer of a righteous man is powerful and effective.*
>
> (James 5:13-16 NIV)

Let us pray for those in hospitals and in mental institutions. Ask the Lord to heal, to deliver and set free. The scripture states how Jesus healed many while He was here on Earth (Matthew 8:16 NIV).

IF YOU ARE SICK, PLEASE PRAY THIS PRAYER NOW AND ASK THE LORD TO HEAL YOU.

DEAR LORD JESUS, THANK YOU FOR DYING ON THE CROSS FOR ME. THANK YOU THAT YOU ARE MY GREAT HEALER. PLEASE TOUCH MY BODY NOW AND HEAL ME OF THIS SICKNESS, I ASK IN YOUR NAME. AMEN!

Governments and leaders: Let us also pray for our governments all over the world. For prime ministers, presidents, ministers of government, councillors and community leaders. They are the ones who make the policies and decisions that affect our lives. Therefore, let us ask the Lord to:

- save those who are not yet saved
- for protection on their lives

- for courage
- for strength
- for wisdom, and understanding
- And for His peace and love to flow in their hearts.

There are many threats to our nations around the world, so let us also pray for our nations. Ask the Lord to deliver those who are in captivity and are oppressed. Pray for those who are tortured and have no hope. Pray for freedom for those nations who are in captivity. Pray for those who are experiencing death and violence that they will come to know the Lord Jesus. We are able to create great changes if we trust in the Lord and call on His name earnestly.

There is a great example in the scripture of King Hezekiah, who prayed to the Lord and saved the nation. King Hezekiah was threatened by the enemy, the King of Assyria, who sent messengers to intimidate him. He told Hezekiah that he would come and take his land, his people and his livestock and destroy them totally. (See 2 Kings 18) But Hezekiah prayed to the Lord for the nation. The scripture says that when he received the letter from the messenger, he went to the temple of the Lord and spread it out before the Lord and prayed to the Lord and the Lord heard his cries and saved them from the threats of their enemies (see 2 Kings 19). God is able to do far more than we can ask or imagine. We are to take everything to Him in prayer.

The apostle Paul knew that leaders and nations need to be prayed for, so he asked Timothy to pray for leaders:

> I urge, then, first of all, that request and prayers, intercession and thanksgiving be made for everyone, for kings and all those in authority, that we may live peaceful and quiet lives in all godliness and holiness. This is good and pleases God our Saviour, who wants all men to be saved and to come to the knowledge of the truth.

> (1 Timothy 2:2-4 NIV)

God is able to deliver us from all evil. The Bible says: *For he will deliver the needy who cry out, and the afflicted who have no one to help. He will take pity on the weak and the needy and save the needy from death* (Psalm 72:12-13 NIV).

The Psalmist declares: *I call to God and the Lord saves me. Evening morning and noon I cry out in distress and he hears my voice* (Psalm 55:16-17).

You may not be able to pray over everything in just one go. Nevertheless, you can make a list and pray over certain things each day. It is also important take the following into consideration as we approach the Lord in prayer:

- to exercise faith
- to always pray in the name of Jesus
- to be consistent
- take time out to fast
- pray everywhere and at all times

Whenever we come before the Lord, it is crucial that we do not come to Him with a guilty conscience. The best way to deal with guilt is to ask Him to forgive us all our faults and mistakes and then we are to believe that He has forgiven us. We should not approach Him feeling condemned and guilty of past mistakes. The scripture tells us that if our hearts do not condemn us, we will have confidence before the Lord. We are to approach the Lord in confidence and believe that He has already forgiven us. He told us that whatever we ask for, He will give us. Therefore, we are to cleanse ourselves before we approach Him and believe in His power to forgive and ask Him for all we need boldly. If we confess our sins, He will forgive us and purify us (1 John 1:9).

Exercise faith: As we pray, we are to believe that God will hear and answer our prayers. Jesus said that whatever we ask for in prayer we are to believe that we will receive it and it will be ours (Mark 11:24). We are also encouraged to ask in faith and do not doubt (James 1:6). If we have faith, we will be able to do what Jesus did.

I tell you the truth, anyone who has faith in me will do what I have been doing. He will do even greater things than these, because I am going to the Father.

And I will do whatever you ask in my name, so that the Son may bring glory to the Father. You may ask me for anything in my name, and I will do it.

(John 14:12-14)

Jesus has given us power, authority, boldness and faith.

Pray in the name of Jesus: Jesus' name is the only way to the Father. We are so privileged to have access to the Father through Jesus. So let us use the name against sickness, diseases, poverty, distress, crime and violence and all the plans of the enemy. He said that He will do whatever we ask in His name: *And I will do whatever you ask in my name, so that the Son may bring glory to the Father* (John 14:13).

He has given us the authority to use His name to ask the Father because He has chosen us: *You did not choose me, but I chose you and appointed you to go and bear fruit, fruit that will last. Then the Father will give you whatever you ask in my name* (John 15:16).

It doesn't matter what state we may find ourselves in, we have got this wonderful privilege to call upon the name of Jesus. Christ has secured the believers' access to our heavenly Father.

We have authority to command changes in this great name. We are to ask for all this in this great name, JESUS. Jesus also said that the Father will give us whatever we ask in His name:

I tell you the truth, my Father will give you whatever you ask in my name. Until now you have not asked for anything in my name. Ask and you will receive and your joy will be complete.

(Luke 16:23-24)

Be consistent: We are to be consistent and persistent as we continue to call upon the name of the Lord. He may not answer our prayers straight away. Nevertheless, He has good reasons to delay our request sometimes. As we persist in prayer our faith will increase in Him and we also grow in Christ. He told us the parable of the persistent widow who never stop until she got what she wanted. It reads:

> *In a certain town there was a judge who neither feared God nor cared about men. And there was a widow in that town that kept coming to him with the plea, "Grant me justice against my adversary."*
>
> *For some time he refused. But finally he said to himself, "Even though I don't fear God or care about men, yet because this widow keeps bothering me, I will see that she gets justice, so that she won't eventually wear me out with her coming!"*
>
> *And the Lord said, "Listen to what the unjust judge says. And will not God bring about justice for his chosen ones, who cry out to Him day and night? Will He keep putting them off? I tell you, He will see that they get justice, and quickly. However, when the Son of Man comes, will he find faith on the earth?"*

(Luke 18:1-8 NIV)

Let us talk to the Lord in prayer as often as you can. Read His Word and never give up, let us pray in the mornings, noon and night and while we are working, walking and eating. He can hear us whenever we call on Him.

Fasting is powerful and useful for all occasions. As we take time to read and pray, we will also have to take time out to fast. Fasting is a time where believers abstain from food and drink and take time out to pray and read God's Word. We fast and pray for various reasons. For example, we fast and make intensive supplication to God to intervene in difficult matters. There are times when we may have to fast and ask for forgiveness, or fast and worship and seek Him for guidance.

There are times in our lives when we will face challenging situations, issues that are tough and seemingly unmoveable and the only way to break these strongholds is through fast and prayer. Many times they will be situations to do with our children, marriages, our nation, our community, sicknesses for souls, difficulties at our work places and many other problems. And many times these situations will only be broken and removed when we take time to fast and pray. Jesus already told us that there are some issues that can only be removed through prayer and fasting (see Matthew 17:21) so it is essential that we take time out to fast and pray.

There are some excellent examples in the scripture of believers who fasted and prayed and saw magnificent changes in their circumstances. For example, when Nehemiah the prophet heard of the ruin of Jerusalem, he sat down and wept for some days and fasted and prayed. The Lord then intervened and He allowed the king to step in and ask Nehemiah what was wrong (Nehemiah. 2:4). The king then allowed Nehemiah time to go to Jerusalem and rebuild the city. (See Nehemiah)

We also read of King Jehoshaphat, the King of Judah, who was threatened by a coalition of nations. But he was not worried by the threat because, he knew that it was limited, but for the great God that he put his confidence in, there is no limit or failure in Him. So he called a nationwide fast and they gave thanks, praised and worshipped the Lord and encouraged the people to have faith in the Lord. And as they called upon the name of the Lord, gave praises and worshipped him, the most amazing thing happened to their enemies. The scripture says that they turned against each other and fought each other (2 Chronicles 20:1-30).

There are all kinds of means that the enemy will try to use to destroy our families and our community, our churches and nation. But we are so privileged that we can take everything to the Lord in prayer and fasting and break all the threats. Take time out to pray and fast for the things that seem impossible. Jesus will honour fasting and work things out for your own good. Jesus Himself fasted forty days and nights (Luke 4:2).

The Bible tells us that the leaders fasted, worshipped and prayed in the church at Antioch and the Lord instructed them. (See Acts 13:2-3) Therefore, we should we should also take time out to fast and pray. Fasting helps us in many ways, such as:

- To focus more on the Lord
- To give more attention to prayer
- To be more self-disciplined
- To break strongholds
- And to gain great experiences and results in prayer.

Many places to pray: There are many places where we can meet to fast and pray. Some meet in churches, some in their homes, some in hotels, some on the streets, some in pubs and some in hospitals and prisons. The scripture shows us how believers gathered in their homes and prayed, as people gathered at Mary's house and prayed for Peter while he was in prison. (Acts 12:12) Solomon prayed in the presence of all the people in Israel (1 Kings 8:22-52).

Many of us have prayer partners, so that we often meet and pray together, maybe weekly or twice per month.

Praying together will help others to find strength, to increase our faith, to be more effective, build self-esteem, confidence and friendship. Jesus said that where two or three are gathered, He will be in the midst (Matt. 18:20).

At some churches there are prayer meetings, sometimes once or twice per week, while in some there are home groups or connect groups which meet weekly and pray together. We can also go on prayer walks, walk on the street and pray for our areas. I have walked in my area and in surrounding areas and prayed. As I pray, I release:

- the spirit of God in the atmosphere
- declare His promises to enlarge my territories
- to give me every place I set my feet on
- And to save souls that are in darkness

We can all take time out sometimes and go on prayer walks. It will help your physical strength and increase your stamina.

PERSONAL EXPERIENCES

Over the years I have experienced many great results through prayers. For example, once my Pastor prayed for me in church. But before he started he said,

"Jasmine, all I can see on you is the favour of God." Then he started praying. And as he started, I could see in the spirit as if he had pulled down something and given it to me and said, "Take this, Jasmine, it's yours."

After the prayer a silver circle appeared around me and I was walking around the church with this shining circle around me, expecting someone to ask me about it, but no one said anything.

I was even expecting Pastor himself to ask me about it after church, but he did not say anything No one could see the awesome experience I had that Sunday morning, only me and Jesus. It was a great experience and I will never forget it; it was a very special day to me in prayer.

I have also seen the Lord work for me in many other areas in my life after others have prayed for me. I have seen Him:

- Heal me.
- Provide a job for me.
- Deliver me from many, many impossible situations.
- Give me guidance.
- And speak to me many times.

I have also seen many believers healed, after they have been prayed for at my place of worship. Many people at my church have experienced the healing power of Jesus after they have been prayed for. Children and babies have been healed. Some people have been healed of cancer, some of backache, some of stroke, some of severe pains and many other ailments. I have seen God heal them all.

HINDRANCES TO PRAYER:

There are many obstacles that can prevent our prayers from being answered. Often we allow negative things to stop us from having a right relationship with the Lord. But we are to remember what the scripture says we are to do. It reads: *In the same way, count yourself dead to sin but alive to God in Christ Jesus. Therefore do not let sin reign in your mortal body so that you obey its evil desire* (Romans 6:11-12).

It is imperative that we rid ourselves of all the obstacles that will hinder our prayers. Some of these are: sin, fear, unforgiveness, family issues, idols, bitterness and wrong motives.

Sin: The scripture tells us that The Israelites allowed sins to separate them from the Lord. *Your iniquities have separated you from your God, your sins have hidden his face from you so that he will not hear you* (Isaiah 59:2). God will not hear us if our lives are filled with sins. If we want Him to hear and answer us, it is our duty to rid ourselves of all sinful activities, ask Him to forgive and be obedient to His Word. Then we can approach Him in prayer.

Fear: We should not allow fear to prevent us from receiving our blessings. If we are afraid to approach the Lord in prayer and are worried about our past sins or afraid to ask the Lord for anything because we are afraid that He has something against us, this can stop our faith and prevent our prayers from being effective. We are to ask for whatever we are in need of without fear. We are to take Him at His Word and remove fear from us, because He has not given us a spirit of fear but of love (2 Timothy 1:7).

Unforgiveness: It is important that we learn to forgive those who hurt us. The scripture mentions clearly the way we are to behave toward others and that we are always to forgive others: *For if you forgive men when they sin against you, your heavenly father will also* *forgive you. But if you do not forgive men their sins, your Father will not forgive your sins. (Matt 6:14-15).* God will reveal to us all the anger, bitterness and hurt that we hold against others. As these are revealed to us, it is important that we take time to forgive and to love as He did. He is love and He also calls us to be like Him.

We are also reminded that if we are offering our gifts, and our brothers and sisters are against us, we are to leave the gift at the altar and go and be reconciled with him. (See Matt. 5:23-25) As we take time to pray, we are to aim to have a good relationship with our Lord and with each other. If there is anyone in the family, at church, or at work that you are not in a good relationship with, you are to forgive them and also ask them to forgive you and as you take this step you will feel much better. *A broken and a contrite heart the Lord will not despise* (Psalm 51:17).

Family issues: A broken relationship in the home between husband and wife can also hinder prayer. (See 1 Peter 3:7) The Bible tells us that our iniquities can separate us.

We are also advised clearly that we are to be filled with kindness, compassion and many other attributes and to forgive.

> *Therefore, as God's chosen people, holy and dearly loved, clothe yourself with compassion, kindness, humility, gentleness and patience. Bear with each other and forgive whatever grievances you may have against one another. Forgive as the Lord forgave you.*

> (Colossians 3:12-13b NIV)

We are also encouraged thus:

> *So let us put away the deeds of darkness and put on the armour of light. Let us behave decently, as in the daytime, not in orgies and drunkenness, not in sexual immorality and debauchery, not in dissension and jealousy. Rather clothe yourselves with*

the Lord Jesus, and do not think how to gratify the desires of the sinful nature.

(Romans 13:12-14 NIV)

As His dear children, let us throw off everything that hinders us and prevent our prayers from been answered.

(Hebrews12:1-2)

Idols*:* Our prayers can be hindered if we give preference to anything over the Lord. We are to love Him first above any things else on this earth. *You are to love the Lord your God with all of your heart, your soul and your strength* (Deuteronomy 6:5). The Lord should take first place in our lives and nothing else. Our idols can be anything: television, our jobs, our cars, children, husbands, wives. Anything to which we give more precedence than the Lord has become our idol. We are to examine our lives daily to see whether anything else takes first place. We are to love the Lord more than anything else. Let Jesus take first place and nothing else.

Bitterness is a dangerous thing. It means that we are holding something against someone. Maybe people have hurt you at work or even in church and you have become bitter against them. But the Word of God warns us that we should not harbour bitterness in our heart or else the Lord will not hear us. *If I regard iniquity in my heart the Lord will not hear me* (Psalms 66:18). We should avoid all iniquity and allow the grace and peace of God to reign in our lives so that our prayers will not be hindered. The scripture shows us how to keep our hearts pure. *Get rid of all bitterness, rage and anger, brawling and slander, along with every form of malice* (Eph. 4:31).

It is dangerous to have bitterness in our hearts. It will stop our prayers from being effective. Let us get rid of bitterness and serve the Lord with a clean and pure heart.

For our prayers to be effective and bring changes to all situations, to heal the sick, cast out demons, raise the dead and help nations, it is imperative that we listen to the astounding warning that Jesus gave us and throw aside everything that hinders us (Hebrews 12) and live a successful Christian life. God is able to give us victory as we follow His Word.

Let us continue to ask without ceasing, pray to God, He is still hearing and answering our prayers.

The scripture says we are to be joyful in hope, patient in affliction, and faithful in prayer (Romans 12:12).

His Word says we are to take everything to Him without being anxious:

> Do not be anxious about anything, but in everything we are to go to God in prayer and petition, with thanks giving and present our request to God.

> (Phil 4:6)

The apostle Paul showed us he prayed intensely for other believers. Ever since he heard of the Colossian believers he did not stop praying for them:

> For this reason, since the day we heard about you, we have not stopped praying for you and asking God to fill you with knowledge of his will through all spiritual wisdom and understanding.

> And we pray this in order that you may live a life worthy of the Lord and may please him in every way: bearing fruit in every good work, growing in the knowledge of God, being strengthened with all power according to his glorious might so that you may have great endurance and patience and joyfully giving thanks to the Father, who has qualified you to share in the in the inheritance of the saints in the kingdom of light. For he has rescued us from the dominion of darkness and

brought us in the kingdom of the Son he loves, in whom we have redemption through his blood the forgiveness of sins.

(Colossians 1:9-14)

The smoke of the incense, together with the prayers of the saint, will go up before God (Revelation 8:4 NIV).

AND PLEASE ALWAYS REMEMBER TO PRAY THE LORD'S PRAYER!

**OUR FATHER IN HEAVEN,
HALLOWED BE YOUR NAME.
YOUR KINGDOM COME.
YOUR WILL BE DONE,
ON EARTH, AS IT IS IN HEAVEN.
GIVE US TODAY OUR DAILY BREAD
FORGIVE US OUR DEBTS,
AS WE ALSO FORGIVE OUR DEBTORS. AND LEAD
US NOT INTO TEMPTATION,
BUT DELIVER US FROM THE EVIL ONE
FOR YOURS IS THE KINGDOM
AND THE POWER AND THE GLORY. AMEN.**

(MATTHEW 6:9-13)

As I finish this chapter on prayer, I will now ask those who do not know the Lord Jesus, to pray this prayer and ask Him to forgive you, and to come into your heart:

DEAR LORD JESUS, PLEASE FORGIVE ME OF ALL MY SINS AND COME INTO MY HEART, I PRAY. AMEN.

Jesus will be happy to hear you and to come into your heart. He is more than able to change your life and to make you into a new person and to continue listening to your prayers.

Chapter Three

BE FAITHFUL IN YOUR GIVING

Our Lord has given us so much that it is only natural that we should want to give Him something back. Giving is mentioned throughout the scriptures. Both the Old and New Testaments make mention of the principle of giving. God is also a giver. In the Old Testament, Nehemiah pointed out how believers gave in the past as follows:

- They gave to the Lord's house first.
- They gave their best.
- They gave a tenth of what they owned.
- They were also promised that they would be blessed and that they should not neglect giving to His house. (See Chapter 10: verses 37-39)

Giving is still necessary for believers today. In many of our churches, tithes and offerings and other gifts are collected. This money is used for various purposes. In some circumstances, it is used to pay ministers or other workers, to help the needy, to assist missionaries and oversee missions and to take care of other expenses. The Lord is expecting us all to give, because we are His children and we are expected to behave like Him. God has already shown us how much He loves us by giving His only Son to die for us, so giving should be a part of every believer's life. As we give Him ourselves first, we are expected to surrender all our possessions to Him and to also give Him our talents, skills and abilities. In the Bible days, the people had to give first to the Lord their precious goods, their tithes and special gifts. Nehemiah wrote about the procedure:

Bring your burnt offerings and sacrifices, your tithes and special gifts, what you have vowed to give and your free will offerings and the firstborn of your herds and flocks. (v:6). Moreover, we will bring to the store rooms of the house of our God, to the priest, the first of our ground meal, of our grain offerings, of the fruit of our trees and of our new wine and oil. And we will bring a tithe of our crops to the Levites, for it is the Levites who collect the tithes in the entire town where we work. A priest descended from Aaron is to accompany the Levites when they receive the tithes, and the Levites are to bring a tent of the tithes up to the house of our God, to the storerooms of the treasury. The people of Israel, including the Levites, are to bring their contributions of grains, new wine and oil to the storerooms where the articles for the sanctuary are kept and where the ministering priests, the gatekeepers and the singers stay. We will not neglect the house of our God.

(Nehemiah 10 37-39 NIV)

These are the many gifts that the believers were asked to give to the house of the Lord. They were advised to give a tenth of what they owned and they were also required to take care of the Levites, who did the work in the Lord's house.

It is the Levites who are to do the work at the Tent of Meeting and bear the responsibility for offences against it. This is a lasting ordinance for the generation to come. They will receive no inheritance among the Israelites. Instead, I give to the Levites as their inheritance the tithes that the Israelites present as an offering to the Lord. That is why I said concerning them: They will have no inheritance among the Israelites. The Lord said to Moses, "Speak to the Levites and say to them: When you receive from the Israelites the tithes I gave you as your inheritance, you must present a tenth of that tithe as the Lord's offering."

(Numbers 18:23-26)

The Hebrews also gave what the owned. They gave their crops, the fruit of the trees and herds and flocks. (See Leviticus 27:32) Stinginess is not encouraged anywhere in the scripture. We are encouraged to give and to share.

It is also mentioned openly in the book of Malachi that we are to bring all the tithes and offerings into His storehouse and in return He will bless us in large quantity. (Malachi 3:10-11)

From what we have observed, believers in the past gave lavishly and generously. It is reported that Hezekiah had to build storerooms in the temple, to store the contributions the people brought as they gave faithfully. (See 2 Chronicles 31:11)

We are expected as followers of Christ to put Him first and to give Him our best. The book of Proverbs tells us that when we give, we will be rewarded. The generous man will prosper, and he who refreshes others will also be refreshed (Proverbs 11:25). In the book of Hebrews we read about Abraham who practised giving. He met Melchizedek, the King of Salem, and gave him one tenth of everything he possessed. (Hebrews 7:1-4) This is a good example for all of us to emulate. Abraham, who is called the father of those who believe and a righteous man, paid his tithes and offering, therefore we are to do the very same.

We also read that when others gave, they received much more than they had given. For example, the Queen of Sheba's action is a great illustration of giving and receiving. The scripture records that the Queen of Sheba heard about King Solomon's wealth and fame and went to see him. But she did not go empty—handed. She took many gifts to him: spices, gold and precious stones, and King Solomon in return gave her much more than she gave. (See 1 Kings 10:10-13) This example demonstrates the power of giving. It shows that giving begets giving, it attracts favour, it demands a response, and it is fitting for all classes and generations.

I have heard some people say that the act of tithing is an Old Testament principle and is not appropriate for today's believers. But the rule of giving still applies to us today. Giving is a proper way of showing how much we love the Lord and others. He shows us how important it is to give by giving first to us. He gave us His only son Jesus. And He wants us to give from our hearts and to give cheerfully. (See 2 Corinthians 9:7)

While Jesus was here on Earth, He did not deny the principle of giving. He gave attention, affection, love, time and kind words. He also mentioned tithing and said that it should not be the only good thing that we should do, but we are to also give attention to other issues.

> *How terrible it will be for you teachers of religious law and Pharisees.*
>
> *Hypocrites! For you are carefree to tithe even the tiniest part of your income, but you ignore the important things of the law, justice, mercy and faith. You should tithe, yes, but you should not leave undone the more important things.*
>
> (Matthew 23:23 NLT)

Jesus also sat and watched those who were giving. He noticed those who gave in abundance, those who gave a small portion and those who gave their all. (See Mark 12:41-44) Jesus also said that we are to give and we will receive great quantity.

> *Give and it shall be given to us. A good measure, pressed down, shaken together and running over, will be poured into your lap. For with the measure you use, it will be measured to you.*
>
> (Luke 6:38)

As we take time out to give, let us aim to give the best of ourselves, our worship, praises, time, talents, skills and money. We should also think of the poor as we give. It is also important that we give kind words and show compassion to all people as Jesus did.

God expects all of us to give to His work. Money is needed in all areas of life. The apostle Paul encouraged the Corinthians that they should aim to excel in their giving (2 Corinthians 8:7). And we also should aim to stand out in our giving. Jesus is expecting us all to give, not just our money, He wants our time, our love and attention to others.

We should also give food and clothes to those who are in need. Jesus provided for thousands of people and fed many in abundance while here on Earth. He also warned the Pharisees that they should give in all circumstances.

> *But how terrible it would be for you Pharisees! For you are careful to tithe even the thinnest part of your income but you completely forget about justice and the love of God. You should tithe, yes, but you should not leave undone the most important things.*

> (Luke 11:42 NLT)

We also read how His disciples wanted the people to go and obtain food for themselves in a difficult circumstance, but Jesus stopped them and advised them to feed the people by themselves. (See Matthew 14:15-21) Jesus gave all to others, His love, time, kind words and food.

Although our churches and the places where we worship need financial assistance, and it is important that we give, we should also give in other circumstances. Yes, money is needed to keep our buildings operating and to pay those who work there. It is also a wonderful thing to be able to give to the Lord. We are privileged to be able to demonstrate how much we love Him by giving to Him. But let us also give to others around us who are in need and to those far away.

In most of our churches believers are asked to give ten per cent of their earnings, which is called tithes. Everyone who is a member of a church is asked to give their tithes and offering. It doesn't matter who you are, whether you are a minister, Sunday school teacher, usher or cleaner, so long as you attend a church regularly you are asked to give, wherever you worship. As I mentioned before, this money is used to pay those who work for and in our churches, pastors, and other workers. They all need to be paid as they spend their time to serve the Lord's purposes. The worker deserves his wage. (See Luke 10-7) This method was also practised in the past. In the Old Testament the people were asked to give tithes to the Levites who worked in the Tent (Numbers 18:21). It is impossible for any of us or for any institution to function without money. We all need money and each other's time, skills and talents.

In some churches people are asked to give first fruit offerings at the beginning of the year. We often give the best of what we have. This money and other gifts are used for many useful purposes. In some cases it is used to purchase musical instruments, furniture or to carry out repairs and to give to others in need.

At my church there are also times when we are asked to give money, food and clothing to distribute to people in our communities. We should cherish these opportunities to show how much we love and care for others. The Lord gives us resources so that we can help others and it is vital that we exercise this great privilege and give willingly to others.

We should give with a good attitude. Giving is a great act of faith. In the Book of Acts the believers followed the principle of giving and they gave plenty. Many gave more than the ten per cent requested of them. Some even sold their lands and houses and gave the money to the apostles and they in turn distributed it to those who were in need. (See Acts 4:33-35)

I am not suggesting that anyone should sell their home and become homeless, only pointing out the enthusiasm and great faith that they displayed in giving in those days. We can all exercise our faith in different ways in our generation and the Lord will always bless us. Paul tells us the attitude we are to display as we give.

Remember this: whoever sows sparingly, will also reap sparingly, and whoever sows generously will also reap generously. Each man should give what he has decided in his heart to be able to make all grace abound to you, so that in all things at all times, having all that you need, you will abound in every good work as it is written: give not reluctantly or under compulsion, for God loves a cheerful giver.

(2 Corinthians 9:6-7)

We are also reminded that God is able to give us more than we can ask for or even imagine.

Now to him who is able to do immeasurable more than we ask or imagine, according to his power that is at work within us.

(Ephesians 3:20 NIV)

It is not wise for us to have an intention to keep all one hundred per cent of what the Lord has blessed us with. We are advised to give ten per cent of what God has blessed us with and the more we give the more we will receive. And we are advised not to store up treasures here on Earth where they can be destroyed and stolen, but we are to store them up in heaven and in God's house, where we can be rewarded (Matthew 6:19-20).

The scripture also warns us, to keep away from all kinds of greed and that our life is not based on the abundance of our possessions. (See Luke12:15) Giving is spiritual sowing and *as we give we will reap* (2 Corinthians 9:7). All that we gain in Life, our Lord has blessed us with. *We brought nothing into this world and we cannot take anything out with us, so let us give willingly* (1 Timothy 6:7).

BLESSINGS WE ARE PROMISED AS WE GIVE

The scripture tells us of the many blessings we will receive as we give:

- We are told that as we give to others, it will open up doors for us and usher us into the presence of greatness. (Proverbs 18:16)
- That the generous man will himself be blessed, for he shares his food with the poor. (Proverbs 22:9).
- Food will be in our houses, and that He will pour out blessings that we will not be able to contain. (See Malachi)

We need Him to protect our resources and to protect us from dangers, to provide for us, to destroy bondages and break financial problems. Whenever we pay our tithes we are sowing the seeds to reap a better lifestyle.

There are many blessings promised to us whenever we are generous as outlined in this passage.

He has scattered abroad his gifts to the poor; his righteousness endures for ever. Now he who supplies seed to the sower and bread for food will also supply, increase your store of seed, and will enlarge the harvest of your righteousness. You will be made rich in every way so that you can be generous on every occasion, and through us generously will result in thanksgiving to God.

This service that you perform is not only supplying the needs of God's people but is also overflowing in many expressions of thanks to God. Because of the service by which you have proved yourself, men will praise God for the obedience that accompanies your confession of the gospel of Christ, and for your generosity in sharing with them and with everyone else. And in their prayers for you their hearts will go out to you, because of the surpassing grace God has given you. Thanks are to God for his indescribable gifts!

(2 Corinthians 9:9-15 NIV)

The more we give to the Lord and to others, the more we will receive both from Him and from others. The earth is His and everything in it. He will also meet all our needs according to His riches (Phil 4:19).

Over the years I have heard believers testified that they have struggled and lost money, because of their disobedient action and refusal to give their tithes. Some have mentioned that they have lost money, experienced break down in appliances, and many, many other misfortunes, when they use their tithes to do other things they ended up spending more. We are to give to the Lord what is rightfully His.

There are many difficult situations that we all have to encounter, especially in this twenty-first century. Our economic has taken a downturn and there are many changes taking place in our world. Some times it does appear difficult to pay our tithes and offerings and to give to others. But, we are to be obedient and pay that portion that belongs to the Lord.

Although we may be experiencing financial difficulties, we are to trust in His Word and rely on Him to provide for us. He promised that He will make ways and it is important that we all believe His Word and give that portion that we are asked to give. Some of us may have lost our jobs, while some may be working part-time and others may be living on benefits. Whatever circumstance we may find ourselves in, it is imperative that we put our trust in Him. We can rely on God in this challenging time to provide for us. He will fulfil His promises to us. He cannot lie. He promises to open the windows and pour out His blessing so great that we will not be able to contain it (Malachi 3:10). He is faithful to His Word.

Jesus is able to step into every situation and bring changes. He did it for Peter and others and He can do it for us. He is able to give us plans to make wealth. God is able to reveal all our talents and abilities to us, so that we can utilise them and be a blessing to ourselves and others. He demonstrated to Peter and the other fishermen that He was capable of doing the impossible. The scripture shows us that these men were discouraged, frustrated, tired and disappointed. Everything looked depressing to them that day, but Jesus stepped into the situation just in time and caused an empty boat to overflow with bounty. As we read the following verses we will see how Jesus changed their lifestyle:

One day, as Jesus was standing by the Lake of Genesee with the people crowding around him and listening to the word of God, he saw at the water's edge two boats, left there by the fishermen, who were washing their nets. He got into one of the boats, the one belonging to Simon, and asked him to put out a little from shore, and then he sat down and taught the people from the boat. When he had finished speaking, he said to Simon, "Put out into deep water, and let down the nets for a catch." Simon answered, "Master, we've worked hard all night and haven't caught anything. But because you say so, I will let down the nets." When they had done so, they caught such a large number of fish that their nets began to break. So they signalled to their partners in the other boats to come and help them, and they came and filled both boats so full that they began to sink. When Simon Peter saw this, he fell at Jesus' knees and said, "Go away from me, Lord; I am a sinful man! For he and all his companions were astonished at the catch of fish they had taken.

(Luke 5:1-9 NIV)

Jesus stepped into an empty boat and turned around a depressing situation into abundance. He is able to provide and to turn around any poverty-stricken situation into wealth. Jesus is bigger than any situation. We cannot say because there is a 'credit crisis' we are not going to carry out his command. It is still our duty to give ten per cent of our resources to His house and also to give to others who are in worse situations than we are.

Many of us are so blessed and we should count our blessings and always give God thanks and praises for His great provision. Whenever He answers our prayers we are blessed. When we ask Him to heal the sick and He hears and answers our prayers we are blessed. When we wake up in the morning and are able to praise Him we are blessed. And we are blessed and privileged when we can tell others about

JESUS. Let's count our blessings and be thankful and obedient to the Lord's Words. As we continue to pay our tithes and offerings and continue to give to others, we will experience His awesome blessings. But if we place obstacles in our way, we can stop the outpouring of our blessings and favours both great and small.

We should all be aware that good things don't always come in big packages. Sometimes they come in small packages. For example, a small voice that says, 'Don't be afraid', or 'I will be with you', or 'I love you and I will provide for you'. These are some of the beautiful things Jesus says and does for us. There are occasions when the Lord will speak to us in our quiet times. These moments can be very uplifting, whenever we hear His voice. We are blessed in so many ways by the Lord.

Giving to Him will place a demand on Him to out-give us and He is more than able to out-give us. He calls us for a purpose, and it is vital that we be obedient to His Word and give. God has no limit to the amount of blessings that He is able to pour out on our lives. We read in the Book of Kings an extraordinary story of God's great provision. It shows how God provided for a widow, an impoverished woman who was indebted and faced with a severe predicament. The scripture tells us that her creditors were threatening to come and take her children and enslave them. When we are indebted, the debt collectors often threaten to come and take our goods, furniture and other assets, which quite frightening enough. But for this woman, they were threatening to take her children! But our great God sent Elisha to her, and he gave her a strategy to deliver her from her dilemma. (See 2 Kings 4:1-7) She obeyed the instruction, and she was able to make wealth and come out of her poverty. God is a great provider, He is the same yesterday, today and forever and His blessings are able to flow to all generations and to transform lives.

This same Lord that provided for a poor widow is also able to provide for us in extraordinary ways. As we give to the Lord, we will experience growth in many areas of our lives: in our churches, both spiritually and numerically, our relationships, our family. We will also gain new territories, excel and be fruitful.

Once I heard an elder at our church say that he felt so blessed whenever he paid his tithes and offerings. There is always a good and pleasant feeling whenever we give. He also said that even when he was unemployed and only receiving benefits, he still honoured God's Word and paid his tithes and today he is such a blessed man, working and serving in the church, flowing in the Spirit and the blessings of the Lord are on him and his family. There are times when circumstances cause us to contemplate and even refuse to give and to pay that portion to the Lord's house. My suggestion is to be obedient and give to the Lord's house and, as you give, speak positive words over your life:

- I am fruitful.
- I have power to gain wealth.
- I will excel at all things.
- I am blessed.
- I can't lose when I give.
- The more I give, the more I gain.

And as you proclaim these powerful words, you will certainly see changes.

CONSEQUENCES WHEN WE REFUSE TO GIVE

In the book of Malachi, the prophet urges the people to stop holding back their tithes and offerings. He ordered them to give to the Lord what is already His. Everything on this earth is the Lord's. He provides us with all the resources so that we can live on this earth. God also gives us strength and skills so that we can obtain wealth. Therefore, as we obtain material blessings, we are to give back a portion to His work. The Bible tells us emphatically that we are under a curse if we refuse to pay our tithes (Malachi 3:9). If we refuse to pay our tithes we are installing barriers to stop His blessings from reaching us. Some of the obstacles we can encounter are strain on our resources, hidden opportunities and fruitless living.

The scripture says that we are robbing God, whenever we refuse to pay our tithes:

Will a man rob God? Yet you rob me. But, you ask, 'how do we rob you?' In tithes and offerings. You are under a curse, the whole nation of you, because you are robbing me.

"Bring the whole tithes into the storehouse. Test me in this," says the Lord Almighty, "and see if I will not throw open the floodgates of heaven and pour out so much blessings that you will not have room enough for it. I will prevent pests from devouring your crops, and the vine in your fields will not cast their fruit," says the Lord Almighty. "Then all the nations will call you blessed, for yours will be a delightful land," says the Lord Almighty.

Malachi 3:6-12 (NIV)

They were also warned that there would be certain penalties if they refused to give to the Lord's house. For example, their crops would be destroyed and they would experience a curse on their lives. (Malachi:3-13)

Disobedience always results in a severe penalty. We read in the Book of Jonah how Jonah disobeyed the Lord's command when he was asked to go to the city of Nineveh. Jonah tried to disobey and ran away, but he experienced a great trauma because of his disobedience. (See Jonah 1) God is omnipresent. He sees and knows about us. He knows all that we do and say. The Bible says that the Lord sent a great wind on the sea. A violent storm started because of Jonah's disobedience. There is always a penalty whenever we refuse to listen and obey God's command.

Whenever we refuse to give, we are depriving other countries of the Good News. Oftentimes missionaries and other leaders depend on financial assistance from the churches to help them to go overseas. Money helps to get the Gospel to others.

Our Lord is able do exceeding abundantly above what we can ask for or even imagine, so let us pay our tithes and experience His abundant blessings. I want to encourage everyone reading this book to practise the habit of giving.

Maybe you are wondering why I am able to speak about tithing and offering so passionately. Well I am, because of my experiences. I never used to pay my tithes and offering as I should have done. But over the years I have learnt my lesson, and become obedient to His Word. It took me some time to be obedient to God's Word. When I first became a Christian, I only used to pay my tithes when it was convenient for me. But during those disobedient years, I felt the consequences. I can remember experiencing losses, setbacks and added bills and expenses. Even though I heard the message preached over and over on tithes and offering, I did not give it priority. I used my money to purchase clothes and to do my own business without taking out that first portion that belonged to the Lord. I later found myself indebted and faced with all kinds of financial difficulties. I had to turn to God's Word and ask Him to forgive me and I started paying my tithes and offering regularly. I would not wish anyone to experience the things I have experienced and the consequences.

Since I started paying my tithes and offering as I should, my whole life has changed: my circumstances changed, my mentality changed and I became more positive. With a better outlook, I could see changes for the better. God is willing to give all of us second chances if we take responsibility for our actions and change. We are to say sorry and start giving to the Lord. I am not a preacher, a pastor, or an evangelist of any church, just a believer in Christ, but over the years I have seen, heard and experienced the consequences of not giving.

This chapter has shown us how the believers of old gave their best and gave in abundance. It also shows how Jesus Himself encouraged giving and gave Himself. Giving is relevant in our world today. We are to aim to give our best, to give to others and to give more than money, both to Him and others.

We can only be successful when we are obedient to God's command. As we give, we will demonstrate our love to the Lord and to others. Giving begets giving and God loves a cheerful giver. Jesus is watching us as we give. We cannot hide from Him. Let's continue to give our best, in love, in faith, willingly both to our churches and to others. It is more blessed to give than to receive.

LIVE A SUCCESSFUL CHRISTIAN LIFE

Chapter Four

BE WILLING TO TELL OTHERS ABOUT THE LORD JESUS

Jesus has called us all His flowers to go and tell the world about Him:

Go into all the world and preach the good news to all creation. Whoever believes and is baptised will be saved, but whoever does not believe will be condemned.

(St. Mark 16:15-16)

He also promised that He will give us the Holy Spirit that will empower us to carry out this great task:

But you will receive power when the Holy Spirit comes on you: and you will be my witness in Jerusalem, and in Judea and in Samaria, and to the ends of the earth.

(Acts 1:8 NIV)

In this chapter we will look at those who have helped to tell about Jesus in the past; consider how we are to prepare to tell about Jesus; what to tell others; where and who to tell about Jesus and the benefits and obstacles we may face.

Maybe you are asking the question, 'Why should I tell others about Jesus?' There are many reasons why we are to spread this Good News about Jesus. But, most importantly, we are to tell others about Him because He said we are to do it. The scripture says we are Christ's ambassadors (2 Corinthians 5:20). He makes His demands through us to take the message to unbelievers. We should tell others about Jesus because He loves and care for people.

Jesus also sent a beautiful invitation to the world that all should hear about:

> *Come to me, all who are burdened, and I will give you rest. Take my yoke upon you and learn from me, for I am gentle and humble in heart, and you will find rest.*

> (Matthew 11:28-29 NIV)

We are the only ones available to take this message to unbelievers and many are dying in sin who need to hear about Jesus. For all these beautiful reasons, it is mandatory for us to tell others about Him. Jesus Himself also spread the Good News:

> *But he said, "I must preach the good news of the Kingdom of God to the other towns, because that is why I was sent." And he kept on preaching in the synagogues of Judah.*

> (Luke 4:43-44 NIV)

Other men and women followed suit and witnessed of Jesus (Luke 2:41). The scripture states that the apostles preached the gospel and crowds gathered to hear and see them. (See Acts 5:12-16). The apostle Paul did remarkable work for the Lord. He spread the message of Jesus. He witnessed and saw many lives changed. (See Acts 17:1-4) He also stated how he felt compelled to spread the gospel (1 Corinthians 9:16) and that the gospel he preached is not made up by man but received by revelation from Jesus Christ (Galatians 1:11-12). He said that his desire was to finish the task the Lord had given to him, the task of testifying the gospel of God's grace (Acts 20:24).

We also have something SPECIAL from the Lord, and we should be delighted to share with others.

None of us will be able to present the Good News well without some form of training. For this reason, it is sensible to take time out to learn something about the subject by reading the Bible and learning about Him, or by listening to others. Although we do not have to be unique in our qualification before we can tell others about Christ. We do not need to be better educated than others, or be a graduate from Bible school. But we are to strive to be more effective in the way we share the Good News. The Lord wants us to be capable in whatever we do. The scripture tells us that God helps us to be excellent in whatever we do. He prunes us whenever we are fruitful, so that we can even be more fruitful. He cuts off every branch in us that bears no fruit, while every branch that does bear fruit He prunes so that it will be even more fruitful. (See John 15:2 NIV) God doesn't want any of us to remain static in whatever we do, but to increase in all areas of our lives. He wants us to improve in our education, in our faith, in our worship, in our jobs and in the way we present the Gospel. For that reason, we are to strive to tell others about Jesus in an efficient way.

Paul tells Timothy that he that he should study the Word so that He will know what it means and be able to tell others about Jesus well, so that he would not be ashamed (2 Timothy 2:15). To be able to explain the scripture correctly, it is vital to take time to study the Bible. Therefore, we are to take time to:

- Learn more about God's Word.
- Learn to fast and pray.
- Learn from other resources.
- Prepare to live exemplary lives.
- Learn from others.
- And learn to accept changes.

The Good News that we will be telling others is a Bible-based message. So, it is important to read and study God's Word and to learn about Jesus. Study the books of the Bible and other elements of the scriptures. Believers should also take advantage of the training sessions that are available in our churches.

There are many training courses in our churches: Bible study courses, courses on how to witness, Alfa courses, also Sunday schools classes for both children and adults in some churches.

We should build our own prayer life as we prepare to tell others about the Lord. Take time to communicate with the Lord and pray about the areas of witnessing, for unbelievers, for love and understanding in the reading, studying, memorising, and the applying of the Word of God. Pray for favour and that hearts may be receptive to the voice of God. Pray for knowledge, wisdom and strength. The apostle Paul wasn't independent of prayer when he was crying out this great mission. He asked the Ephesians believers to pray for him that whenever he opened his mouth, he would be brave, to tell of the mystery of the gospel. (See Ephesians 6:19). He also asked for prayers that the message be spread rapidly all over the world (2 Thessalonians 3:1). Although none of us is able to save anyone yet, we are all responsible to pray and ask the Lord to make a difference in people's lives. Prayer and fasting are key elements for us to practise as we witness to others.

There are many other resources which we can all learn from: CDs, DVDs, Christian literature and preaching. These are Christian resources available to increase our knowledge and help to empower us to be better able to help others to come to know Jesus. As we learn we will be better at what we do. Timothy was advised to be the best at what he did (2 Timothy 2:15). We are to aim to do our best for Christ. Only Jesus can save people. But we can present Him to unbelievers in an excellent manner.

As we prepare to tell others about Jesus, we are to strive to lead exemplary lives, so that people can see how Jesus makes a big difference in our lives. The Bible says we should conduct ourselves in a manner that is worthy of the gospel of Christ (Philippians 1:27 NIV). We are to set examples in our homes, in our work places, on the street, in the marketplace and wherever we are. Many times we may find ourselves in places where we are the only Christian. For that reason, we should let the light of Jesus shine through us with our love, kind words, compassion, forgiveness and peace. Be wise in the way you act to toward outsiders; make your conversation refined (see Colossians 4:5-6). Many times we may not verbalise the message before others recognise who we are, just because of the difference Jesus made in us. They will recognise the warmth, love, compassion, peace and kindness that flow from us. Our actions will show others that Jesus lives because we are in fellowship with Him. We are here to give flavour.

> *You are the salt of the earth. But if the salt loses its saltiness, how can it be made salty again? It is no longer good for anything, except to be thrown out and be trampled by men.*

(Matthew 5:13)

On the other hand, if at any time you happen to make any mistakes, no matter what it is, do not turn away from the Lord. You should NEVER turn away from the Lord, no matter what! You should ask Him to forgive you. Say sorry to Him and to others and continue to do His work. There is power in his name to forgive us for all our sins.

The Holy Spirit is also a powerful source that we are to rely on to strengthen us, to give us insight, so that we will be able to tell unbelievers about Jesus in a magnificent way. It is important that we ask the Lord to fill us with the Holy Spirit as we witness. The Holy Spirit is here for all believers, the scripture says. We are to ask for it and whenever it comes it will teach us all things. (See John 14:25) The Holy Spirit is able to reveal things to us that no other force can do. (See John 16:13)

As we tell others about Jesus we should make it simple. Paul advised us that we are to present the gospel to others in a clear and basic way. We are present it

- in our own style
- in our own language
- and make it simple

We do not have to try to be like others, but be ourselves. Depend on the Holy Spirit to do great works in you and in unbelievers' lives. And as they hear about Christ through us, the Spirit will fire up the message and magnificent things will take place in their hearts.

Telling others about Christ does not entail long or fine words. It is not great works or action that will save others; Jesus is the only one who can save people. We are also advised not to deceive others, but to say what the Word says and to speak about Christ and not about ourselves or our abilities and accomplishments (2 Corinthians 4:1-4 NIV).

It is also necessary to attend to other believers who have been in the church before us. Some have had many, many years of experience and gained a deep knowledge about the Lord. You can tap into their knowledge, find out what they have learnt over the years and learn from them. Some of them already have witnessed to their families, husbands, wives, friends and others, and have seen them accepted by the Lord. We can all learn from each other. Believers are able to give guidance and encouragement; they all have something to offer. (See Proverbs 25:12)

As we share the Good News, let us be willing to accept changes, both young and old. None of us should condition our minds to do things the same way year after year. Society is always changing and people also change. We may have to change some of our methods. For example, we cannot speak to people as those believers spoke two hundred years ago or continue to use some of the words used in older versions of the Bible. Even language changes, so we should prepare to change and adapt. Many new technologies are available to aid us to spread the Good News more powerfully. We aim to use them and to learn about the ones with which we are unfamiliar. Some ways to tell others about Jesus are: the telephone, the internet, Twitter, email, Facebook and the other media. Jesus wants others to come to Him and, whatever system we can use, we are to utilise it. There are no excuses in this generation not to spread the Good News. This is the reason why Jesus came to earth. Christ came into the world to save sinners. (See 1 Timothy 1:15) God holds us responsible for unbelievers who are around us. Our Lord and His angels are pleased when others hear about Him and come into a relationship with Him. We have all the tools to let everyone know about Jesus. Let's not be responsible for those who do not hear the Gospel. Ezekiel says, *'When I say to a wicked man, "You will surely die," and you do not warn him or speak out to dissuade him from his evil ways in order to save his life, that wicked man will die for his sin, and I will hold you to account for his blood* (Ezekiel 3:18 NIV).

As we tell others about Jesus, let us aim to bring out the best in people:

- be positive
- communicate well
- be polite to others
- be warm with others; smile, shake hands and be approachable
- do not be judgemental

If possible, invite people for lunch or coffee and tell them about this book! And always display a sense of humour. Do not bully anyone into accepting the message. Salvation is something that only God can give. Do not disrespect others or treat them as inferiors. Do not be arrogant or proud. We were also sinners.

> *We were foolish at one time, disobedient, deceived and enslaved by all kinds of passion and pleasure. We lived in malice and envy, being hated and hating one another.*

> (Titus 3:3)

Jesus came into our lives and changed us and He will do the same for others, so be patient with unbelievers.

Jesus said, if people do not want to listen to us we are to shake off the very dust and leave them (Luke 9:5 NIV). We also have the example of Paul. He shook out his clothes and left Corinth, whilst preaching the Gospel.

> *But when the Jews opposed Paul and became abusive, he shook out his clothes in protest and said to them, "Your blood be on your own head! I am clear of my responsibility. From now on I will go to the Gentiles."*
>
> (Acts 18:6 NIV)

Whatever the circumstance, we should not force anyone. Do this work effectively. We can all do it well if we take time to educate ourselves about the topic, fast and pray and trust in God, and leave the rest in His hands.

Many times believers erect all kinds of barriers that prevent them from witnessing to others. Some have said that:

- They are not as clever as others.
- They are not as holy as others.
- They are not experienced as others.
- They do not have the time.
- They are not competent enough.
- They are not worthy—and many more excuses.

Whatever barrier we may erect, none should prevent us from speaking about the Lord. Jesus called us to tell others about Him, and we are more than able to tell someone about Him. There is always someone around us to share Jesus' love with.

WHAT SHOULD WE TELL OTHERS?

Jesus did so much while He was here on Earth and so much in our own lives. We have so many praises and good deeds to tell others about Him. We are also chosen to carry out this magnificent duty of telling others about this great King.

*But you are a chosen people, a royal priesthood, a holy nation, a people belonging to God, that you may declare the **PRAISES** of him who called you out of darkness into his wonderful light.*

(1 Peter 2:9 NIV)

Nevertheless, it is wise to begin this task by telling others of the difference Jesus made in your own life. Your experience is unique and, as you tell others your story, people will be thrilled to hear it. So you are to tell others what you were like before you came to know Jesus. Many will realise how powerful Jesus is and will be eager to have a relationship with Him. Your testimonies are exceptional and people will be more willing to listen to you than to someone merely quoting scriptures. People will remember your story for a very long time.

I have heard many exciting, life-changing stories in our churches. Many believers and unbelievers have been moved by them. Some have even come to know the Lord Jesus after they have seen the change in people.

For example, some spoke of their involvement in crime, drugs, murder and told how they had been on death row. But Jesus stepped in and transformed seemingly hopeless situations. These mighty powers move people to come to Jesus. Some of us had financial or family worries, broken marriages, when everything looked hopeless. Yet Jesus saved us and transformed our circumstances. We can all tell others of His goodness. Some of us have also seen our children delivered from drugs, crime, illegal activities and prison. Now we can share these things with others. Having seen changes, some are serving the Lord, some are in leadership positions, others working. These are excellent testimonies to tell others. Some people tell how Jesus has healed them from cancer and other life-threatening diseases and now they are healed and in His house, worshipping and praising Him. God has taught us so much from disappointments, failure, sorrow and waiting. We all have something to tell.

Peter said we are to be prepared to give an answer to everyone who asks us about our hope (1 Peter 3:15). Jesus himself preached while He was here. (See Matthew 4:23-24) We have more than enough to share and to help others to come to know the Lord Jesus. He has done so much for this world, and some of us have experienced so much in Christ, that I am sure we can all share something from what we have heard, seen and read about Him.

However, if you are still contemplating what to say, here is a list of some of the magnificent works and promises from the scripture that you can share with unbelievers. He has made many promises and others need to hear about them.

- Jesus loves them.
- Our Lord Jesus promised that all those who come to Him, will inherit eternal life (John 3:16).
- Jesus paid the penalty for our sins (Romans 6:23).
- While we were sinners Christ died for us (Romans 5:8).

You can tell others of His saving power.

Salvation is found in no one else, for there is no other name under heaven given to men by which we must be saved (Acts 4:12).

- His ability to forgive sins. If we confess our sin He is able to forgive us. (1 John 1:9).
- He did not come to earth to call the righteous but sinners. (See Matt. 9:13)
- You can tell others that God has called us into fellowship with Him (1 Corinthians 1:9).
- He gives us freedom (Galatians 5:13).
- Jesus gives us hope (Ephesians 1:18).
- Tell others that we all belong to Jesus, and He calls all of us out of darkness into His marvellous light (1 Peter 2:9).
- Tell others that Jesus is the only Ruler, King of kings, Lord of lords and is immortal (1 Timothy 6:15-16).
- He is Lord and Saviour. (Luke 24:48)

- He is the author and finisher of our faith (Hebrews 12:2).
- He is crowned with glory and honour (Hebrews 2:9).
- You can also tell others of Jesus' birth His birth is unique. The Bible explains His miraculous conception and how Mary His mother was visited by the Angel who told her that she would have a child while she was still a virgin. (See Luke 1:26-36 NIV)
- You can tell others how He healed the sick (Matthew 4:23) and how He taught and empowered His disciples (Matthew:5 1-12).

You can tell others how He did things that seem impossible:

- He walked on water. (See Mark 6:45-51)
- He changed water into wine (John 2:1-11).

Jesus died on the cross for us. (See Matthew 27:41-44) He was also raised from the dead (see Mark 5:42-43) and He is gone to prepare a place for us and He is coming back again (John 14:2-3 NIV).

We can go on and on talking about Jesus; there is no boundary to His greatness and power. There is so much to tell about Him, so continue to:

Tell of His: anointing, tell of His blessings, tell of His compassion, tell of His deliverance, tell of His everlasting grace, tell of His goodness, tell of His holiness, tell of His impartiality, tell of His joy, tell of His kindness, tell of His love, tell of His mercy, tell of His nearness, tell of His omnipotence, tell of His peace, tell of His qualities, tell of His righteousness, tell of His saving grace, tell of His tenderness, tell of His unfailing love, tell of His victories, tell of His wonderful works, tell of His excellent life, tell of His years on earth and tell of His Zeal.

We are great witness and are chosen. *"You are my witnesses," declares the Lord, "my servant whom I have chosen, so that you may know and believe me and understand that I am he. Before me no god was formed, nor there one after me"* (Isaiah 43:10 NIV).

WHERE AND WHO SHOULD WE TELL?

Jesus our Lord tells us that we are to

> *Go into the entire world and preach the good news to all creation. Whoever believes and is baptised will be saved, but whoever does not believe will be condemned. And these signs will accompany those who believe. In my name they will drive out demons; they will speak in new tongues; they will pick up snakes with their hands; and when they drink deadly poison, it will not hurt them at all; they will place their hands on sick people, and they will get well.*
>
> (Mark 16:15-18 NIV)

Many of us will not be able to go all over the world to start this mission. Nevertheless, we do not have to travel far to start telling others about the Lord Jesus. We can all start wherever we are. There are many places we can go and witness to others. Some of us may not be able to travel to the seven continents or appear on television and radio as others do. But we can tell those who are close by us. We can start telling others about Christ right where we are and, as the opportunity arises, we can go further and further. The disciples started telling others just where they were. Day after day, in the temple courts, from house to house, they never stopped teaching and preaching the Good News that Jesus is the Christ. (Acts 2, 3, 4) The scripture says that the Lord showed Philip, the Ethiopian eunuch who was close by him. Philip obeyed the Spirit of the Lord and went and spoke to him and he accepted the Lord Jesus. (See Acts 5:25-40)

There are many people around us who do not know the Lord. We should share Him with them, our family, our neighbours, our friends and those we work with.

Some of us will find ourselves in positions where we can speak to large groups of people and people of influence. Some of us may have a desire to become politicians, to travel the world, to be great sportsmen and women, to be actresses or journalists, while some may want to care for the homeless, children who have been neglected, women who have been abused, men who have been raped. Wherever we are, we are to tell others about Jesus. As you serve in these areas and show love, compassion, kindness and understanding, others will see Christ in you and want to hear about Him. Many may not want to hear because of the awful experiences they have been through. But, show love; be understanding, be kind and allow Jesus to do the impossible. He is able to make the impossible become possible. And He can use you in all areas. He has a way to open up doors in places that seems impossible, so that we can show off His glory. Grab the opportunity and spread the GOOD NEWS!

We should also tell those who are in hospital, in prison and those in other places of confinement. I know that it is not always appropriate to spread the message in some workplaces and especially in this country (England). I am not encouraging anyone to break the law. Still, there are many other opportunities we can find to tell them of His greatness. Do not STOP communicating His blessings to the world. We should not give up. W should not stay silent, but speak about Him in all places. Tell people about Him on the buses, in the streets, in the shops, in the marketplaces, restaurants, at social meetings. Use all avenues to spread the Good News, wherever He sends you and with whomever He sends you to. (See Acts 5:42 NIV)

There are times when the Lord sends us just to one person to do something great, and there are times when He will send us to a group. For example, Jesus sent out seventy-two of His followers to spread the Good News (Luke 10:1-2 NIV). Another time, He allowed just one person to enter a city and speak about Him. We read in the Book of Acts where one man, Philip, a follower of Christ, went to the city of Samaria, where he preached and did many amazing things. The scripture says that the crowds followed Him, he worked many miracles and signs, and he cast out evil spirits. The crippled and paralysed were healed and he also brought joy and hopes to many lives (Acts 8:4-8). He was able to do excellent work by himself, because of the great power of God in him. We can all do something for the kingdom and we can all experience magnificent results because of the great power that is in us. We should aim to be submissive and trust in Jesus fully. The Bible says that many people came to know the Lord Jesus through Philip's preaching: *But when they believed Philip as he preached the good news of the kingdom of God and the name of Jesus Christ, they were baptised, both men and women. Simon himself believed and was baptised. And he followed Philip everywhere, astonished by the great signs and miracles he saw* (Acts 8:12-13 NIV).

This is excellent work carried out by just one man.

Jesus also sent out groups of people to go and spread the Good News and change lives. Peter and John went out together and they healed the sick, told others about the Lord Jesus and won many souls for Christ. (See Acts:3, 4). Paul and Barnabas went to many, many parts of the world and spread the good News about the Lord Jesus (See Acts:13, 14, 15, and 20). God also calls and sends groups.

Maybe the Lord is speaking to a group of people just now: maybe a group of young people or a group of older folks, a group of women or a group of men. He can be calling this group for a very long time to take the step and go and tell somebody about Him. I just want to encourage you to listen, be obedient and take the step and start telling others about Him. Start praying and ask the Lord to guide you and help you to be able to work with others and to give your best. There are many souls to be saved and we need to win them out of darkness and hopelessness into the light of Christ. Those who do not know Him will have to hear about Him through you. We all came to know the Lord Jesus through someone else's words. Somebody shared Jesus with us, and our lives were transformed. It is time for us to stir and share Jesus with others. Ezekiel mentions that the word of the Lord came to him to preach and to prophesy. (Ezekiel 20:45-46). This is one of the main reasons why He called us to preach to others and to prophesy of His immensity.

It is our duty to let others hear about Him in the entire world. *This gospel of the Kingdom will be preached in the world as a testimony to all nations, and then the end will come* (Matthew 24:14 NIV).

It doesn't matter what race, sex, colour, age social class you are or what job title you may have or what mistakes you have made. He is calling YOU! He wants us all to become winners and champions and win souls for the kingdom. The enemy wants the best of us to keep us in captivity to KILL, STEAL and DESTROY our lives. (See John 10:10) Jesus wants us to do great works, and to give us an abundant life.

Let's spread the Good News. He wants those who do not know Him to hear and come to Him.

- Jesus wants the broken-hearted.
- Jesus wants the convicted prisoner.
- Jesus wants the desolate, destitute, deprived and depressed.
- Jesus wants the evil worker, the envious, egotistic and energetic.
- Jesus wants the fornicator, foreigners and fire-fighters.
- Jesus wants the gun-man, gamblers and garbage collectors.
- Jesus wants the homeless, hopeless and happy.
- Jesus wants the illiterate, ill-mannered and ill.
- Jesus wants those in the jail houses, the jobless and the Jehovah's Witnesses.
- Jesus wants the king, the kind-hearted and the killer.
- Jesus wants the lame, the loveless and the loved.
- Jesus wants the malicious, murderers and the mind-readers.
- Jesus wants those who feel as if they are nothing, those who are noble and noteworthy.
- Jesus wants those who are on death-row, outrageous, and outnumbered.
- Jesus wants the poor, the prostitute and the persecuted.
- Jesus wants the queen and the qualified.
- Jesus wants the rich, the robbers and the rejected.
- Jesus wants the simple, the slow learners and the sinners.
- Jesus wants those who are troubled, traumatized and tearful.
- Jesus wants those who are unemployed.

- Jesus wants those who are victorious, victims and violated.
- Jesus wants those who are weak, weary and wanted.
- Jesus wants those who x-offenders.
- Jesus wants those who are young.
- Jesus wants those who are zealous.

God wants us all to follow Him and to tell everyone about Him. *God made him who had no sin to be sin for us, so that in him we might become the righteousness of God.* (2 Corinthians 5:21). Those who are good, He wants us to be better, to be more helpful and competent in whatever we do, even those who are bad and have failed Him in many ways. He wants to make us exceptional, productive and fit for all purposes. He doesn't want us to waste away and perish, but to realise who He is and come and serve Him and help to spread the Good News about Him. We have to tell the world about Him so that no one will be lost. We can all be saved. *For the grace of God that brings salvation has appeared to all men* (Titus 2:11). The Good News is for the poor, the captive, the broken-hearted.

> *The Spirit of the Sovereign Lord is on me, because the Lord has anointed me to preach good news to the poor. He has sent me to bind up the broken-hearted, to proclaim freedom for the captives and release from darkness for the prisoner, to proclaim the year of the Lord's favour and the day of vengeance of our God, to comfort all those who mourn, and provide for those who grieve in Zion—to bestow on them a crown of beauty instead of ashes, the oil of gladness instead of mourning, and a garment of praise instead of a spirit of despair. They will be called oaks of righteousness, a planting of the Lord for the display of his splendour.*
>
> (Isaiah 61:1-3 NIV)

If you are reading this book and you don't know Jesus I am speaking to YOU! I want YOU to know that He loves YOU! And that He gave His life for YOU. YOU are very special to Him. YOU ARE A SPECIAL PERSON! He wants you to have a relationship with Him TODAY! If you ask Him to come into your heart, change your life He is willing to accept you RIGHT NOW! AND MAKE YOU INTO A NEW, VIBRANT PERSON! SAY YES TO HIM!

Jesus says: *Behold I stand at the door and knock; if anyone hears my voice and opens the door, I will come in to him and eat with him and he me* (Rev 3:20).

THE BENEFITS WE WILL RECEIVE

- It is a great honour to be used by God and to become partners in building the Kingdom here on earth.
- The apostle Paul said that we have become co-workers together with God (2 Corinthians 1:6).
- We are very privileged to be able to help to transform lives, to help others to mature and grow in Christ.
- We will also be helping to train the next generation to love and serve the Lord Jesus.
- Many of us will also train up leaders, winners and over-comers.
- As we carry out all this great work, Jesus promised that He will bless us. *He will bless us with all spiritual blessings* (Ephesians 1:3)

We will experience spiritual, physical, and emotional changes in our lives. The scripture mentions that those who come in His name are blessed (Psalm 118:26). We will also experience a thrill when others come to know Him. We will have a sense of worth, satisfaction and accomplishment as we do this great mission. The scripture said that *he who wins souls is wise* (Proverbs 11:30). As you tell others about Jesus you will see situations change: the sick will be healed, the dumb will speak, souls will come to know the Lord, families will be restored, the dead will be raised. His Word declares that *No eye has seen and no ears have heard, or conceived what God has prepared for those who love Him* (1 Corn. 2:9). You will have magnificent value and self-worth as you carry out this task.

OBSTACLES WE MAY FACE AS WE TELL OTHERS

We are all aware that we are not promised a life free from problems and worries and as we share the Good News of Salvation there are many obstructions we will encounter. The scripture also tells us that the gods of this world will try to prevent the Good News from spreading. Paul wrote:

> *The gods of this world have blinded the minds of unbelievers, so that they cannot see the light of the gospel of the glory of Christ, who is the image of God. For we do not preach ourselves, but Jesus Christ as Lord, and ourselves as your servants for Jesus' sake. For God who said, "Let light shine out of darkness", made His light shine in our hearts to give us the light of the knowledge of the glory of God in the face of Christ. But we have this treasure in jars of clay to show that this all-surpassing power is from God and not from us* (2 Corinthians 4:4-7).

Many of us will face obstacles, some of us will be rejected. We will be criticized, ostracized, abused verbally, physically and emotionally. Sometimes we may encounter other obstacles such as fear, ill health, financial strain, family worries, ignorance and distance. But despite all the obstacles, we are called to do His work and we are to be courageous. Maybe at times you will have to abandon your agenda and accept God's.

Jesus, Paul and many others who were spreading the gospel experienced difficulties. They had trials, suffering and distress. But they did not allow anything to stop them. Paul outlined some of the suffering he went through. He said that he was flogged, exposed to death, stoned and experienced shipwreck. He spent night and day on the open sea. He also experienced difficulties with other brothers and sisters, and he was thirsty, hungry and naked. (See 2 Corinthians 11:23-28)

We can see that others did not have it easy, as they told about the Lord Jesus, and we won't find it easy to spread the Good News. We will face problems; sometimes we will feel like giving up. Don't let the pain of criticism stop you from telling others about the King. Allow the resurrection power of Christ to strengthen you moment by moment and spread the Good News. Sometimes we may become dispirited because people have not responded, or things did not work out the way we planned. Even so, we are to take courage, and tell others about the Lord Jesus. We are humans and humans can be discouraged, but we should not give up. (Acts 18-9:10 NIV)

Jesus was rejected and jeered at while He was on Earth, yet he did not give up. He went from place to place and proclaimed the Good News. We are His followers, and we are to set the example for others to follow. He already set the example for us to follow. Many men and women are still spreading the Good News of salvation in our world today. Many face challenges; some have even lost their lives. Yet all these challenges have not stopped believers from talking about the Lord Jesus. He promised us that he will never leave us, and that He will hear us when we call. Let's trust in Him to help us to be bold and tell others about Him.

Let no obstacles stop us from telling others about Jesus. Jesus is in our hearts, so let nothing shut us up! Tell others about Him. Let no fear stop you, no mistakes, no criticism, no problems: tell the world who Jesus is! Nothing can stop Jesus from moving on this earth. He is too powerful to be prevented by anyone or any evil forces. In the Book of Matthew, we read how the enemy tried to stop Jesus, even after His death. The enemy is always trying to prevent Him in life and in death but He managed to overcome all barriers. The scripture mentions that they conducted meetings, met with priests, tried to secure the tomb, posted guards and made every effort to stop Jesus. (Matthew 27:62-66) But He broke through that concrete and came back to life. He is the same today: nothing can stop Him from working for us, His children. We need to tell the world how mighty Jesus is. Nothing can stop Him from working in His children's lives, no situation, no rock, no leader, no problems, no security—nothing can stop Him from saving His people.

EVERYBODY NEEDS TO KNOW WHO JESUS IS!

Tell the Good News to the **A**mbulance worker, tell the **B**arber, tell the **C**leaner, tell the **D**entist, tell the **E**ngineer, tell the **F**armer, tell the **G**ardener, tell the **H**airdresser, tell the **I**nspector, tell the **J**udge, tell the **K**ing, tell the **L**awyer, tell the **M**echanic, tell the **N**urse, tell the **O**ptician, tell the **P**olice, tell the **Q**ueen, tell the **R**eceptionist, tell the **S**oldier, tell the **T**eacher, tell the **U**niversity student, tell the **V**et, tell the **W**aitress, tell the **X**-offender, tell the **Y**oung person, and tell the **Z**oologist.

Chapter Five

HAVING FAITH IN GOD

And without faith it is impossible to please God, because anyone who comes to him must believe that He exists and that He rewards those who earnestly seek Him (Romans 11:6 NIV).

It is a fundamental principle that all believers exercise faith in the Lord. As the above scripture states, without faith it is impossible for us to please Him. Interestingly, believers have always exercised faith in God. The scripture tells us of some of the astounding ways they have put their trust in the Lord (see Hebrews 11) and have seen Him worked magnificently.

Although the word **faith** was not used frequently in the Old Testament, it was faith that these believers were exercising. They were mainly asked to trust in God. But it carries the same meaning and also gives the same glorious result in both the Old and New Testaments. For example, they were encouraged to trust in the Lord, as it reads: *Trust in the Lord and do good; dwell in the land and enjoy safe pasture* (Psalms 37:3).

They were also warned not to trust in idols (Isaiah 42:17), but to trust in the Lord with all their hearts (Proverbs 3:5).

This chapter will discuss:

- the types of faith past believers displayed
- how Jesus dealt with people of faith

- the various ways that we can exercise faith in God
- and the many scriptures we can apply to strengthen our faith in the Lord

The Bible tells us of many great men and women who displayed tremendous faith in God. It outlines how many acted on their faith by obeying God's Word, spoke positively, worked tirelessly and had exceptional results. Some of these people were Abel, Abraham, Enoch, Noah, Sarah, Isaac, Jacob and Rahab. (See Hebrews 11) These men and women were outstanding in the way they put their trust in the Lord. I will now elaborate on the actions of some of these great people of faith.

Abel was an excellent example of a man of faith; he was commended for the great gifts he offered to God. The Bible says:

> *By faith Abel offered God a better sacrifice than Cain did. By faith he was commended as a righteous man, when God spoke well of his offerings. And by faith he still speaks, even though he is dead.*

(Hebrews11:4)

He exercised great faith in God by giving his best to Him. He offered a better sacrifice than his brother Cain. The Bible says, *Abel brought fat portions from some of his firstborn, and the Lord looked with favour on his offering* (Genesis 4:4). Because of Abel's faith and generosity, he was highly praised as a righteous man. This tells us that our faith in God will stir us to give our best to the Lord. Jesus gave His best and we should also give our best.

> *I tell you the truth, anyone who has faith in me will do what I have been doing. He will even do greater things than these because I am going to the father.*

(John 14:12 NIV)

Abraham was also an excellent model of faith. He listened to God; he did not question Him when the Lord called him. The Lord called him to leave his people, his land, friends and comfort and to go to Canaan. Abraham obeyed God's calling; he took everything and left. That was a great act of faith. He believed that God would protect him, provide for him, guide him and keep him in perfect peace. He obeyed the Lord, and there were no regrets in his actions.

> The Lord said to Abram, "Leave your country, your people and your father's household and go to the land I will show you. I will make you into a great nation and I will bless you, I will make your name great, and you will be a blessing. I will bless those who bless you and whoever curses you I will curse; and all people on earth will be blessed through you."

> So Abram left, as the Lord had told him and Lot went with him. Abram was seventy-five years old when he set out from Haran. He took his wife, Sarai, his nephew, Lot, all the possessions they had accumulated and the people they had acquired in Haran, and they set out for the land of Canaan, and they arrived there.

> (Genesis 12:1-5 (NIV)

We also read about **Enoch**, how he lived a life to please God and he was taken up in heaven. He did not experience death. He was commended as one who pleased God. Without faith it is impossible to please God. As we serve the Lord and follow His command, love Him, worship Him, and exercise faith in Him, we will please the Him. (See Hebrews 11:5-6) Enoch lived a life that pleased the Lord. He exercised faith in his God by obeying His word. The Lord wants us all to live exemplary lives to please Him in our daily walk with Him. *Enoch walked with God; then he was no more, because God took him away* (Genesis 5:24).

Noah was another great example. He is described as one who obeyed God, and had faith and confidence in Him. Noah did not follow the ungodly principles in his time, but was righteous in God's eyes. Noah was instructed to build an ark which would save him and his family.

Noah was a righteous man, blameless among the people of his time, and he walked with God. Now the earth was corrupt in God's sight and was full of violence. God saw how corrupt the earth had become, for all the people on earth had corrupted their ways. So God said to Noah, I am going to put an end to all people, for the earth is filled with violence because of them. I am surely going to destroy both them and the earth. So make yourself an ark of cypress wood; make room in it and coat it with pitch inside and out.

(Genesis 6:9, 10-4)

Noah obeyed the Lord's instruction and through his act of faith, his life and his whole family's lives were saved.

Isaac: We also read how Isaac exercised faith in God. When there was a famine in the land of Gerar, Isaac wanted to leave and go to Egypt. But the Lord appeared to him and told him **not** to leave the land, but to stay and He would bless him. Isaac wanted to run away from the famine, but the Lord told him to stay where he was and receive His blessings. (See Genesis, 26:2-69) Many times we may want to run away, because of difficult situations and circumstances that confront us. Some of us have even contemplated suicide to escape worries; others may emigrate, some may want just to run away and hide. But Jesus does not want any of us to run away, but to lean on Him. He is able to bless and provide for us wherever we are, if we exercise faith in Him. He is able to bless us, right where we are. Nothing is too big or too small for Him. The earth is His and everything in it. The Lord worked out a great situation for Isaac and He is able to do the same for you. Isaac saw the threat of famine, hunger, worries and depression. But God saw a way to step in and defeat the apparently hopeless situation. And Isaac obeyed God's Word and exercised faith in His promises and he was blessed abundantly. The Bible says that *Isaac planted crops in that land and the same year reaped a hundredfold, because the Lord blessed him. The man became rich* *and his wealth continued to grow until he became very wealthy. He had many flocks and herds and servants that the Philistines envied him* (Genesis 26:12-13).

It is vital that we exercise faith in God in our generation. Many of our actions are acts of faith already, For example, we took an act of faith and ask Jesus to come into our life. We did not see the Lord with our physical eyes, neither did we touch Him. But many of us came to know just by listening to someone speak about Him, or we may have read about Him. Then we accepted Him in our hearts as Lord and Saviour of our lives. This is a great act of faith But, this process doesn't stop there; it is a continuous process. Jesus is looking for us to display continuous faith in Him. He wants us believe in Him for all things, to act when He speaks to us or calls us and our Lord can call any of us in the twenty-first century to do extraordinary work for Him any moment. Just as He called Noah, Abraham and the others in their generation He can call you.

Maybe the Lord is speaking to **YOU! JUST YOU, READING THIS BOOK!** He may be telling you to step out of your comfort zone, and start building in your generation just as He told Noah to step out and build something big. He may be telling you likewise, maybe to:

- rebuild destitute lives
- build mansions
- build homes for others
- build schools
- build hospitals
- build churches
- and build a better world! How about this!

I just want to advise you to be obedient to the call and step out in **FAITH** and do what He is telling you! The Lord promised that He will be with us always. Jesus is able to give us all the resources that we may need to carry out this great task. He will also give you wisdom, strength and favour in all that you venture out to do. Jesus tells us that we can do awesome things if we have faith. (See Matthew 21:21) So please, step out, by faith and start building if He is speaking to you. He wants you to expand and He also wants lives, cities, towns and neighbourhoods to expand through you.

The Lord told Abraham to leave his homeland and go to another country. He was told to leave his family, his town, his friends and his security and to go. Maybe God is also telling you NOW to leave where you are, and to go elsewhere. Maybe He is calling you in one of the following areas. Do not resist Him. He is still speaking to people today and He can be telling you to:

- go to another country
- go into hospitals and prisons
- go on mission
- go and speak to your neighbours
- go and sing and bring others to Him
- go leave a life of sin
- become a Member of Parliament
- become a president or leader

Some may be called to become prime ministers. There are many areas that we may be called to serve in. Do not be disobedient! Trust in Him to be with you. He will not disappoint any of His children. The most important thing to do is to step out in faith and believe in Him. He will always prove Himself to us. He is well able to supply all our needs, to guide, to protect us and to enlarge us in all areas of our lives. He has helped others in the past and He will do the same for us today. AMEN!

At times the callings on our lives may appear bigger than us. Sometimes, they may look impossible. And many of us may even see ourselves as inferior. But remember that nothing is impossible with the Lord.

Often times some of us make excuses, and sometimes we worry about our family, finances, education, abilities and so on. Jesus told us not to worry. (See John 14) We should not worry about what we will eat or wear, because our life is more than food and He will provide for us. We are to have faith in Him and to seek His Kingdom. (See Luke

12:22-32) Abraham and others forsook all and followed Him. He did not disappoint any of them, but He blessed them and expanded their territories. God is in charge of every thing. Whenever He speaks, it is essential that we listen and be obedient. *If we are willing and obedient, we will eat the best from the land* (Isaiah 1:19).

The Psalmist also declares how fulfilling it is to be doing the work of God:

> *Better is one day in your courts than a thousand elsewhere; I would rather be a doorkeeper in the house of my God than dwell in the tents of the wicked. For the Lord God is a sun and a shield; the Lord bestows favour and honour. No good things does he withhold from those whose walk is blameless.*
>
> (Psalm 84:10-11NIV)

The Lord is also calling us out of sin. If you are reading this book and you have not yet accepted Him as your Lord, He is calling you to leave your life of **sin** and to come and have a relationship with Him. He is calling all those who don't know Him in this generation to take a step of faith and come and have fellowship with Jesus today. Ask Him to come into your heart and change your life TODAY! It does not matter how deep you may feel you are in sin. Jesus is able to reach down and rescue you in the deepest and worst situation that you may find yourself in. He is able to save all of us. He is the Saviour of the world. Jesus died so that we can be saved. He gave His life for us so that we can be delivered from the bondages of sin.

> *For God so loved the world that He gave His only Begotten Son, that whoever believes in Him shall not perish but have eternal life.*
>
> (John 3:16 NIV)

You can take a step of faith and ask Jesus to deliver you today. The Bible says: *Today, if you hear His voice, do not harden your hearts* (Hebrews 3:15 NIV)

PLEASE PRAY THIS PRAYER TO HIM AND ASK HIM TO SAVE YOU TODAY!

DEAR LORD, THANK YOU FOR SENDING YOUR SON TO DIE FOR MY SINS. THANK YOU FOR LOVING ME. PLEASE FORGIVE ME OF ALL MY SINS. COME INTO MY HEART, LORD JESUS, SAVE ME LORD, WASH AWAY ALL MY SINS AND MAKE ME A NEW PERSON. THANK YOU, LORD, FOR WHAT YOU HAVE DONE IN MY LIFE TODAY. AMEN.

This is all you need to do, to accept Jesus. Just ask Him by faith to come into your heart and save you and he will be more than willing to answer your prayer. Whenever God calls us, all we need to do is say yes to Him and pray and ask Him by faith to forgive us and to come into our hearts. He is always willing to receive us. Whenever He calls us, His aims are to bless us, to transform our lives and to give us eternal life. This is the only way you can be saved.

If you are a follower of Christ, you can also take a step of **faith** and ask the Lord to save your loved ones and the nation at this moment. He is able to do all things. Whatever you ask in His name, He will do it. Ask Him to change and bless those who are closest to you and the nation. He is able to do all things if you ask Him by faith today.

He called Abraham and told him that He would bless him and make him into a great nation, and make his name great. This is what God will do for you and your family and friends if you exercise faith in Him. He will bless you and make you great. Those who trust in the Lord will be like Mount Zion, which cannot be shaken but endures for ever (Psalm 125:1). His Word also declares: *The Lord is good to all: he has compassion on all He has made* (Psalm 145:9).

Although the Lord calls some of us to leave where we are and to go elsewhere, there are also times when He will request that we stay just where we are and exercise faith in Him and be blessed. He told Isaac to stay where he was and promised that He would bless him. (See Genesis:26) Isaac wanted to leave where he was, because of the famine. (See Genesis 26:12) But God chose to bless him just where he was. God can tell us to stay where we are and to start up businesses, to speak to those around us, to build our community, and to serve those around us and wait on Him.

Nevertheless, while we are waiting to experience blessings, we are to do something. Some of the things we can do as we exercise faith are to read and obey His Word, pray and speak His Word over our situations, pay our tithes and offerings and give to others. We should also build ourselves up by doing courses, speak to others who are more knowledgeable, improve our skills and abilities and have great expectations as faith and works go together.

For example, if you are thinking of setting up a business, read books on management and leadership, ask questions about starting up your own business, talk to those who have their own businesses and pray and speak positive words. Faith without action is useless (James 2:20). God is also able to give us ideas, to make wealth so that we can help ourselves and others. His Word tells us that He can give us the ability to produce wealth.

> *But remember the Lord your God, for it is He who gives you ability to produce wealth.*

> (Deuteronomy 8:18a)

Exercise faith in God, and take steps and do something with our hands, our mind and our intellect while we are waiting. Isaac did not sit and look at the famine or sit and complain; he worked, planted crops and he reaped a harvest.

HOW DID JESUS DEAL WITH PEOPLE'S FAITH?

Jesus our Lord met many people of faith during His time here on Earth, and He dealt with them in different ways. He complimented some for their faith, He was often surprised at the level of faith that some people displayed and He rebuked others who lacked faith. For example, the scripture tells us of the woman who was suffering with severe bleeding for twelve years. She had also spent all her money on doctors, but was not cured. But after she met the Lord Jesus, she reached out by faith and touched His garment and she was healed immediately. (See Luke 8:43-48) Jesus complimented her for the tremendous level of faith she displayed. He was able to tell her that her faith had made her well. We also read of the centurion who had great faith in the Lord Jesus, so that he asked Jesus not to come to his house to heal his child, but to speak the word and his child would be made well. Jesus was amazed at his level of faith. (See Luke 7:1-10) Many amazing works have been accomplished because people exercised faith in the Lord. Jesus also had to rebuke His disciples, because they did not exercise their faith (Matthew 8:26).

Jesus met many who had faith in Him and he wants us to exercise faith in Him in this era in all areas of our life. The scripture tells us of the powerful defence that we have in Him:

The Lord is my rock, my fortress and my deliverer; my God is my rock, in which I take refuge. He is my shield and the horn of my salvation, my stronghold.

(Psalm 18:2)

As we have been assured of such a magnificent defence, it is essential for us to develop our faith in Him for everything. The only way we can develop our faith in God is by reading, speaking and believing His Word. Why? Because faith comes by hearing the message and the message is heard through the word of Christ (Romans 10:17). There are many areas in our lives where we are to build our faith. We should never become defeated or discouraged because of life issues, but to exercise faith in the Lord Jesus, even though some of our needs, wants and expectations may not come to us straight away. Nevertheless, we are to take courage, speak positive words, be patient and have faith for Him to work in all theses areas. We are to exercise:

FAITH IN TIMES OF DIFFICULTIES: There are times in our lives when we will face all kinds of challenging circumstances. We may be burdened by grief, overwhelmed by sorrows, beaten by death, disaster, sickness and all kinds of troubles. Many believers, myself included, have been through many "fiery" experiences in the past. I have seen many going through painful all-consuming experiences. Some have lost their children, some have lost their jobs. For some, their health has deteriorated and others have lost their parents. It is not an easy road we are travelling. There are pains, stresses and grief. Nevertheless, we are to employ faith in everything. God promised to carry us through. The Psalmist says:

Though you have made me see troubles, many bitter, you will restore my life again; from the depths of the earth you will again bring me up. You will increase my honour and comfort me once again.

(Psalm 71:21-21 NIV)

God has helped others and He is able to help us. Remember, He says: never will I leave you, never will I forsake you. Despite all the trials, troubles and pain that we may encounter in life, we are to stand firm in our faith, not to give up on our faith in Him and trust in Him to strengthen us in our difficulties. Paul told the Corinthians about the excellent comfort that we all can obtain from God:

Praise be to the God and Father of our Lord Jesus Christ, the Father of compassion and the God of all comfort, who comforts us in all our troubles, so that we can comfort those in any trouble with the comfort we ourselves have received from God.

(2 Corinthians 1:3-4 NIV)

We should never forget the one we place our trust and confidence in, the one who created everything; His name is Jesus! He is able to do all things. In times of trouble and temptation, act on your faith! Give all to Jesus; trust Him fully. Jesus is able to strengthen us. He says: *Do not let your heart be troubled. Trust in God: Trust also in me* (John 14:1). Jesus rebuked the storm and created calm in people's lives. (See Matthew 8:23-27). If we exercise faith in Him, He is able to calm all the difficulties in our lives.

FAITH TO RECEIVE AND OPERATE IN THE GIFTS OF GOD: As we walk with Christ it is central that we exercise faith in Him to receive and operate in the gifts that He has promised to us. The scripture tells us that we are to: *Pursue love and desire spiritual gifts but especially that you may prophesy* (1 Corinthians 14:1).

> *We have different gifts according to the grace given us. If a man's gift is prophesying, let him use it in proportion to his faith. If it is serving, let him serve, if it is teaching, let him teach, if it is encouraging, let him encourage, if it is contributing to the needs of others, let him give generously, if it is leadership, let him govern others diligently, if it is showing mercy, let him do it cheerfully.*
>
> (Romans 12:6-8)

FAITH IN SPIRITUAL WARFARE: We should exercise faith against spiritual warfare. The enemy always wants to destroy our faith, so let's be strong and take up the shield of faith and fight all his plans (Ephesians 6:16). He also promised that no weapon that is formed against us will ever prosper (Isaiah 54:17). The apostle Paul congratulated the Ephesians because of their great faith.

> *For this reason, even since I heard about your faith in the Lord Jesus and your love for all the saints, I have not stopped giving thanks for you, remembering you in my prayers. I keep asking that the God of our Lord Jesus Christ, the glorious Father, may give you the spirit of wisdom and that the eyes of your heart may be enlightened in order that you may know the hope to which He has called you, the riches of His glorious inheritance in the saints, and His incomparable great power for us who believe. That power is like the working of His mighty strength, which He exerted in Christ when He raised Him from the dead and seated Him in His right hand in the heavenly realms.*
>
> (Ephesians 1:15-20 NIV)

OUR MINISTRY AND MISSION: We are all called to serve in different ministries in our churches. As I have stated before, there are times when our calling may appear so big; bigger than us. Nevertheless, we are to exercise faith in Him to guide and to bless us. *Praise be the God and Father of our Lord Jesus Christ, who has blessed us with all spiritual blessing in Christ* (Ephesians 1:3).

He promised that He will direct our path and He knows what we are capable of. He made us, He knows all about us. Have faith and confidence in Him, to guide us in our ministry. *Being confident of this that he who has begun a good work in you will carry it on to completion until the day of Jesus Christ* (Philippians 1:6).

Whatever ministry He may call you to serve in, have faith in Him to guide you, to give you understanding and to strengthen you and to give you favour. If you are worried about finance, He already promised to provide for us, to feed and clothe us if we only have faith in Him.

> *Therefore I tell you, do not worry about your life, what you will eat or drink; or about your body, what you will wear. Is not life more important than food, and the body more important than clothes? Look at the birds of the air; they do not sow or reap or store away in barns, and yet your heavenly father feeds them. Are you not much more valuable than they?*
>
> (Matthew 6:25-26)

Paul also mentioned the struggles he had been through while he was doing his ministry, but he said he had fought a good fight, and he had kept the faith (2 Timothy 3:7). And that the Lord was with him and graciously gave him all things.

> *What then, shall we say in response to this? If God is for us, who can be against us? He did not spare His own son, but gave Him up for us all. How will He not also, along with Him, graciously give us all things?*
>
> (Romans 8:31-32)

SANCTIFICATION AND CHRISTIAN GROWTH: As we follow the Lord on our Christian journey it is imperative that we take time to read, meditate, repeat and believe in the Lord to strengthen us. Faith comes by us having His Word in us and there are many promises in the scripture to bless and increase us on our journey with Him, such as the following:

Grace and peace be multiplied to you in the knowledge of God and of Jesus our Lord, as has His divine power given to us all things that pertain to life and godliness, through the knowledge of Him who called us by glory and virtue. By which have been given to us exceedingly great and precious promises that through these you may be partakers of the divine nature, having escaped the corruption that is in the world through lust.

(2 Peter 1:2-4)

May God himself, the God of peace, sanctify you through and through. May your whole spirit, soul and body be kept blameless at the coming of our Lord Jesus

(1 Thessialonians 5:23)

So then, just as you receive Christ Jesus as Lord, continue to live in him, root and build up in him, strengthened in the faith as you were taught and overflowing with thanksgivings.

(Colossians 2:6-7 NIV)

OUR FAMILY SITUATIONS: It is also necessary that we exercise faith and confidence in God to save, guide and protect our families. It is the Lord's desire to see families come to Him and be saved. Paul told the jailer that he was to: *Believe in the Lord Jesus and he and his household would be saved* (Acts 16:31). It is important to have faith and confidence in the Lord to guide and protect our children, that they will best serve the Lord and fulfil their purposes in life.

Although the devil wants to kill and destroy, God is able to do all good things for us.

> *What shall we say in response to this? If God is for us, who can be against us? He who did not spare his own Son, but gave him up for us all, how will he not also, along with him, graciously give us all things?*
>
> (Romans 31-32 NIV)

Jesus is more than able to do all things for us if we exercise faith in Him. Parents should also endeavour to have God's Word in their hearts and to speak God's Word to every difficult issue in their family. We are to speak positive words that will elevate family; speak positive words, especially to the children, that will build their self-esteem and confidence. If your child is at a negative place at this moment, start speaking words of faith and expect their lives to be changed. Start telling your child what the Lord says about him or her. He says and promises all good things and parents are to always speak good words to their children in faith Tell them:

- They were born to serve the Lord.
- They are favoured.
- They belong to the Lord.
- They are special.
- They are leaders.
- And that they will be successful.
- Tell them that Jesus loves them.

As we speak by faith, His Word will manifest in their lives. Tell them what God created them to be in spite of what you may see. Speak positive words. *The tongue has the power of life and death* (Proverbs 18:21). God is able to do immeasurably more than what we can think or speak. *He who is able to do immeasurably more than all we ask or imagine, according to His power that is at work within us* (Ephesians 3:20 NIV).

Stand firm in your faith (Isaiah 7:9b).

FAITH FOR SUCCESSFUL MARRIAGES: We should also have faith in God to make prosper marriages. He wants husbands to love their wives and treat them as the great person they are. He also wants wives to respect, honour and build up their husbands, and for husband and wife to be faithful to each other. We are to believe that all these blessings will be over marriages. There are now so many divorces and separation. But Jesus wants marriages to be successful and for love to flow between husband and wife. He wants all things to work out for His own good. Start speaking to Him and invite Him to take first place in your marriage and to be the head. It is very important that you both speak positive words to each other, words of hope, words of life, words to cheer each other up. Do positive things to change circumstances for the better, work on marriage, start praying, make an effort to change mind sets, start reading His Word and expect situations to change. There are many powerful scriptures that you can read and say to each other and have faith in His Word for things to work out well: Proverbs 31, Mark 10, Colossians 3:18, 1 Peter 3.

Read these words and apply them to your marriage: *Jesus laid down His life for all of us because He loves us* (John 10:14). HAVE FAITH IN HIM TO SAVE YOUR MARRIAGE!

FAITH IN HIM TO SUPPLY ALL OUR NEEDS: The Lord wants us to be blessed in all areas of our lives. He is able to bless us financially and to supply all our needs. *And my God shall supply all your need according to his riches in glory by Christ Jesus* (Philippians 4:19).

He said we should not worry about what to eat or wear but to have faith in Him to provide for us:

> *Then Jesus said to his disciples, "Therefore I tell you, do not worry about your life, what you will eat or about your body, what you will wear. Life is more than food, and the body more than clothes. Consider the ravens: they do not sow or reap, they have no storeroom or barn, yet God feeds them. And how much more valuable you are than birds! Who of you by*

worrying can add a single hour to his life? Since you cannot do this very little thing why do you worry about the rest?

(Luke 12:22-25)

God is able to provide for us and it is important that we trust in Him to provide (Luke 12:22-31).

His Word says: *Beloved, I pray that you may prosper in all things and be in health, just as your soul prospers* (3 John 1:2 NKJV).

The Lord wants to see His children prosper and flourish, although we won't all become millionaires. But in spite of all that is happening, He wants us to live comfortable lives. His promised that He will make us flourish and prosperous as we serve Him.

The righteous will flourish like a palm tree, they will grow like a cedar of Lebanon planted in the house of the Lord, they will flourish in the courts of our God. They will still bear fruit in old age; they will stay fresh and green.

(Psalm 92:12-14)

Everything belongs to the Lord. *The silver is mine and the gold is mine, declares the Lord Almighty* (Haggai 2:8 NIV). We are to seek Him and have faith in Him to show us how to obtain our portion of silver and gold. And as the Lord blesses us with money, we should also assist others in need. (See James 2:14)

The Lord is also willing to bless us financially, but as He gives money to us, we should always remember to pay our tithes and offerings. The Bible says: *the love of money is the root of evil* (1 Timothy 6:10). However, the lack of money can cause depression, fear, frustration, low self-esteem and worry. None of us should ignore the financial aspects of our life as we exercise faith in God. God is not limited in His resources, ideas and knowledge. The following is an example of a person who exercised limited faith in God's provision. In the Book of Kings we read about the widow who was told to collect bottles and to start pouring the oil she had in her house. But though she exercised faith in doing what she was told to do, she collected a limited amount of bottles. The number of containers she gathered was an indication of her faith. God's provision is larger than our faith. We are to think big, and make plans and place no limit on God. He is able to step in and do awesome works for us. (See 2 Kings:4)

FAITH FOR HEALING: We are often faced with all kinds of sickness and disease in this life. But we can all exercise faith in the Lord Jesus to heal us from all sickness and disease. He spoke words of faith, He reached out and touched others, and others touched Him by faith and received their healing. The scripture tell us:

> *Surely he took our infirmities, and carried our sorrows, yet we considered him stricken by God, smitten by him, and afflicted. But he was pierced for our transgression, he was crushed for our iniquities; the punishment that brought us peace was upon him and by his wound we are healed.*

(Isaiah 53:4-5 NIV)

For example, the Centurion exercised great faith in the Lord's healing power *(Matthew 8:5-10)*.

There are times we may have to press in spite of the illness that we face. There are many examples where people took action and received their healing. They cried out to Jesus, they moved to where He was, they touched Him, they followed Him, they were persistent, they had faith and had confidence in His healing power and they received their healing. People will sometimes try to discourage us. Let no one stop you from crying out to Jesus for your healing. Have faith. The Psalmist says: I *love the Lord, for He heard my voice. He heard my cry for mercy. Because He turned His ears to me, I will call on Him as long as I live* (Psalm 116:1-2).

There are many scriptures that tell us that the Lord is able and willing to heal us.

Bless the Lord, O my soul, and all that is within me, bless his holy name! Bless the Lord O my soul, and forget not all His benefits: Who forgives all your diseases (Psalm 103:1-3).

I have had my own experience of His healing power manifested in my life as already mentioned in Chapter One, by me calling upon His name and repeating healing scriptures over myself.

FAITH IN GOD TO BLESS OUR COUNTRY: Whichever country you may live in and whatever may be happening, you are to trust in God for deliverance. He is able to do all things. He knows all that is taking place and He is able to bring deliverance. In many countries there is killing, corruption, unfairness, injustice, and all kinds of crimes. Nevertheless, we are to ask the Lord Jesus to bless and deliver our country. His Word declares that we are to:

Trust in the Lord and do well; dwell in the land and enjoy safe pasture. Delight yourself in the Lord and he will give you the desires of your heart.

Commit yourself to him and he will do this: He will make your righteousness shine like the dawn, the justness of your cause like the noonday sun. Be still before the Lord and wait patiently for him; do not fret when men succeed in their ways, when they carry out their wicked schemes. Refrain from anger and turn from wrath; do not fret, it leads only to evil. For evil men will be cut off, but those who hope in the Lord will inherit the land.

(Psalms 37:3-9 NIV)

He also tells us that:

If my people who are called by my name will humble themselves and pray and seek my face and turn from their wicked ways, then will I hear from heaven and will forgive their sin and will heal their land.

(2 Chronicles 7:14)

We all need to see changes in our world. In our infrastructure and superstructure, God is able to do great things in all areas as we exercise faith in Him.

And the Lord has declared this day that you are his people, his treasured possession, as he promised that you are to keep all his commands. He has declared that he will keep you in praise, fame and honour, high above all the nations, he has made and that you will be a people holy to the Lord your God, as he promised.

(Deuteronomy 26:18-19 NIV)

FAITH IN ALL OTHER AREAS: Having faith in God doesn't mean that we won't go through fire, but in spite of all these challenges, impediments and difficulties, that we may encounter, remember that Jesus is always with us. The scripture shows how important it is to have confidence in the Lord. Whenever we are faced with any impossible situations, we are to take courage and take time out to read His Word and believe it. Only by us plunging into His Word and believing in it will we experience changes. *Jesus is the author and finisher of our faith* (Hebrews 12:2).

It is our responsibility to have positive faith in Him. Jesus has already shown us His principles to trust in Him. Just as those believers in the early days believed in God and were successful, we, too, should trust in Him totally. Let's be determined and say, like the apostle Paul, that neither death nor life, neither angels nor demons, neither the present nor the future, nor any powers, neither height nor depth, nor anything else in all creation, will be able to separate us from the love of Christ. (Romans 8:38-39) As we love and follow Him, we will trust Him to do all things for us and lift up our eyes to Him and know that our help comes from Him (Psalm 121:1-8) and put our hope and confidence in His Word. The scripture says:

Therefore everyone who hears these words of mine and puts them into practice is like a wise man who builds his house on a rock. The rain came down, the streams rose, and the winds blew and beat against the house; yet it did not fall, because it had its foundation on the rock.

But everyone who hears these words of mine and does not put them into practice is like a foolish man who built his house on sand. The rain came down, the streams rose, and the winds blew and beat against the house, and it fell with a great crash.

Matthew 7:24-27 (NIV)

Let us build a strong foundation in Him, by being obedient to His Word.

James also tells us that as we exercise faith we should also exercise deeds:

What good is it, my brothers, if a man claims to have faith but has no deeds? Can such faith save him? Suppose a brother or a sister is without clothes and daily food? If one of you says to him, "Go, I wish you well; keep warm and well fed," but does nothing about his physical needs, what good is it? In the same way, faith by itself, if it is not accompanied by action, is dead. But someone will say, "You have faith; I have deeds." Show me your faith without deeds, and I will show you my faith by what I do. You believe that there is one God. Good! Even the demons believe that and shudder. You foolish man, do you want evidence that faith without deeds is useless?

Was not our ancestor Abraham considered righteous for what he did when he offered his son Isaac on the altar?

You see that his faith and his actions were working together, and his faith was made complete by what he did. And the scripture was fulfilled that says, "Abraham believed God, and it was credited to him as righteousness, and he was called God's friend." You see that a person is justified by what he does and not by faith alone. In the same way, was not even Rahab the prostitute considered righteous for what she did when she gave

lodging to the spies and sent them off in a different direction?
As the body without the spirit is dead, so faith without deeds
is dead.

Let us continue to develop positive attitudes, to speak positively and think and act positively. God wants us to be people of faith. Those around us will also feel better and they will learn to exercise faith in the Lord themselves.

We should remember the many great promises and comforting words of faith to us:

- We are justified by faith.
- We live by faith.
- Those who have faith have been blessed along with Abraham, the man of faith.
- You have been saved through faith.
- We can reach unity through faith.
- You can encourage others in the faith.
- We are to pursue faith.
- We are to excel in faith.
- We are to stand firm in the faith.
- By faith the walls of Jericho fell down.
- Faith and deeds work together.
- Without faith, it is impossible to please God.

These pages have demonstrated the many ways faith can work in our lives. They explain how believers in the past exercised their faith in God and seen The Lord work in many ways. Their faith allowed them to receive provision, to receive healing and salvation, to see the dead rise. They also mention the many areas where we are to exercise faith in God. But in spite of the negatativity in our world today, they also show that having faith in the twenty-first century is still essential and is able to work today as it did in biblical times.

So let's have faith in Him to: **a**ccompany us on our journey, have faith in Him to **b**less us, have faith in Him to **c**omfort us, have faith in Him to **d**irect us, have faith in Him to **e**nlarge our territories, have faith in

Him to **f**orgive us, have faith in Him to **g**uide us, have faith in Him to **h**eal us, have faith in Him to **i**nstruct us, have faith in Him to help us to find **j**obs, have faith in Him to **k**eep us, have faith in Him to **l**ead us, have faith in Him to **m**eet our needs, have faith in Him to be **n**ear us, have faith in Him to **o**pen up doors for us, have faith in Him to **p**rovide and **p**rotect us, have faith in Him to **q**uicken us, have faith in Him to **r**estore us, have faith in Him to **t**each us, have faith in Him to **u**nite us, have faith in Him to give us **v**ictory, have faith in Him to **w**atch over us, have faith in Him to help us to perform excellent work, and have faith in Him to bring the devil to **Z**ero.

LET'S HAVE FAITH IN GOD!

Chapter Six

SAY 'NO' TO SIN!

Sin has been around from the beginning of time, and it still exists today. Sin is disobedience to God's holy laws. Whenever we commit sin, we violate what the Lord demands of us. Often our actions will result in severe consequences, such as shame, regrets, exclusion, fear and condemnation.

In the book of Genesis we read how Adam and Eve sinned by disobeying the Lord's commands. This resulted in a severe penalty for both, because they were expelled from the Garden of Eden. The relationship they had with the Lord also changed and the whole human race was affected by their actions. Sin is destructive and will hinder us from being successful in our walk with Christ. We are to be obedient to God's laws and say no to sin.

The scripture warns believers and non-believers how crucial it is to stay away from sin. The Bible clearly states that we should no longer continue with the former actions, attitudes and ways that fight against our souls, but are to live good lives, so that others will see and glorify God. (See 1Peter 2:11) After we have become followers of Christ, it doesn't mean we won't be tempted to sin. Sometimes temptation even seems greater than before we became believers. The most important thing to remember is that we are all chosen and we all belong to the Lord and it is crucial that we aim to please Him and continue to SAY 'NO' TO SIN. *No one who continues to sin has either seen him or knows him* (1 John 3:4-6 NIV).

None of us is exempt from making mistakes. Both Christians and non-Christians make mistakes and, as Christians, if we claim that we are without sin, we are deceiving ourselves and the truth is not in us (1 John 1:8). But none of us should allow sin to dominate our lives. We are advised not to allow sin to reign in us, and we are to count ourselves as being dead to sin. The scripture declares that:

> *In the same way, count yourself dead to sin but alive to God in Christ Jesus. Therefore do not let sin reign in your mortal body so that you obey its evil desires. Do not offer the parts of your body to sin, as instruments of wickedness, but rather offer yourselves to God, as those who have been brought from death to life, and offer the parts of your body to him as instruments of righteousness. For sin shall not be your master, because you are not under law but under grace.*

(Romans 6:11-14 NIV)

Jesus did something great for us and we should allow **HIM** to reign in us. He gave His precious life on the cross for us (John 3:16). And now He wants us all to remain grateful and continually to say, serve Him, truthfully. Through Christ's death, He destroyed the devil's power and set us free who were held in slavery to sin. (See Hebrews 2:14-15)

The message that I wish to share with those who have not yet accepted Jesus as their Lord and Saviour is that He is waiting for you to be brave and step out and say 'yes' to Him. It is essential that you ask Him to come into your life and make a difference by turning your life around for His glory.

He wants us to inherit everlasting life and to have peace. He also wants us to show His love and to have dominion in our daily lives. Many people have already taken this brave step and accepted Him as their Lord and Saviour. We have been baptised in water and are walking with Him. Unfortunately, many are still grieving Him and committing all kinds of sinful acts which are displeasing to Him. Whenever sin presents itself, the Lord still requires the believer always to say 'NO' TO SIN. Jesus is waiting for the non-believer to turn away from a life of sin and to accept Him as Lord of their life. So, if you are reading this book and you have not yet accepted Jesus as the Lord and Saviour of your life, then pause and think about it. Ask the Father to forgive you of all your sins and to save you. After making this life-changing decision, I am recommending that you attend a church regularly which teaches you how to maintain your relationship with the Lord Jesus. It is also important that you then ask to be baptised. (See Matthew 3:6) You can now continue to read His Word, walk in His way and continue to say 'NO' TO SIN!

Let Jesus be your closest and dearest friend, because He promised that He will never leave you or forsake you. The Bible says: *In Him we have deliverance through His blood, the forgiveness of sins, in accordance with the riches of God's grace* (Ephesians 1:7).

This is the only way we can live a productive, successful Christian life. By loving Him, remaining in Him and serving Him for the rest our lives and keep SAYING 'NO' TO SIN!

There are many sins that the scripture cautious us to keep away from. Jesus used astonishing language to stress how important it is **not** to encourage sin in our lives. (See Mark 9:43-45)

The following are some of the attitudes that we are warned to stay clear of:

Anger: Anger is a strong emotion that we feel when someone behaves in a cruel and unacceptable way toward us. But the Word of God cautions us to control our anger and warns us not to remain angry with others or it could result with us being judged by the Lord. *But I tell you that anyone who is angry with his brother without cause will be subject to judgement* (Matthew 5:22).

We are also advised to control our anger and not to allow the sun to go down on it (Ephesians 4:26). The scripture also says that: *We should not sin by letting anger gain control but we are to think about it overnight and remain silent* (Psalms 4:4 NLT).

Let us search our hearts and endeavour to keep them clean and pure before the Lord. Be quick to listen, slow to speak and slow to become angry. *Anger does not bring about the spiritual fruits that God desires us to possess* (James 1:19-20). It is essential that we conduct ourselves in a manner worthy of the gospel of Christ and get rid of all anger (Ephesians 4:31).

Bitterness: Bitterness is a feeling of revenge. We can all feel bitter and angry when others hurt us, but the scripture advises us not to allow any bitterness to dwell in us. *See to it that no one misses the grace of God and that no bitter roots grow up to cause trouble and defile many* (Hebrews 12:15 NIV). Peter told Simon the Sorcerer that he was full of bitterness and a captive to sin. (See Acts 8:23) We should not let any form of bitterness capture us into the snare of sin; instead, we are to say 'no' to bitterness.

Covetousness: Covetousness is the desire to have something that belongs to someone else. But, we should not covet our neighbour's house, wife, servant or anything that belongs to others. (See Exodus 20:17)

Covetousness is unacceptable. (See Romans 13:9) Sin will encourage us to be covetous and we should avoid it. God is more than able to bless all of us. He is well able to give us all that we need.

Disobedience: Disobedience is deliberately not doing what someone tells you to do. The Bible warns us not to be disobedient, because every disobedient act comes with consequences. Because of the disobedience of one man, many were made sinners. (See Romans 5:19) Disobedience has affected the whole human race. It is very important that we are obedient to the Lord whenever He speaks to us. Being obedient to the Lord brings benefits from the Lord that come with rewards and blessings when we sincerely obey Him.

Evil: Evil refers to all the wicked and bad things that happen in the world. It is an unpleasant and harmful activity. We should put to death all evil desires. (See Colossians. 3:5)

Fornication: Fornication means to have sex with someone that you are not married to. Fornication is sex outside of marriage and it is detested in the Word of God. The Word of God states that we are to stay away from sexual sins. If we are to be effective in our Christian walk, we should aim to put aside sexual activities and to allow Christ to reign in us. We are to be holy, as Christ is holy. The Lord Jesus lives inside of us and He cannot reign in vessels that are unclean. We are the temple of the Lord (1 Corinthians 6:19). We are to flee from sexual immorality (1 Corinthians 6:13-19). Let's say 'no' to all forms of sinful sexual activities. God promised that He will judge the adulterer and all types of sexually immorality (Hebrews 13:4).

Greed: Greed is the desire to have more than necessary. We are to refuse to be greedy and at the same time we should try to develop an attitude of sharing with those who have nothing; in other words, we should develop a desire to help those who are in need. The apostle Paul mentions that some are filled with all kinds of greed. (See Romans 1:29) Such activities should not be encouraged. (See Colossians 3:5) Let's not fall into the sin of greed and condemnation. Let us be honest, upright citizens.

Hatred: Hatred is an extremely strong feeling of dislike for someone. We are told that hatred stirs up conflict and we are to use love to cover all offences. (See Proverbs 10:12) God wants us to love each other and not to destroy our lives and others with hatred. (See Galatians 5:20)

Idol Worshiping: We should be careful not to worship anyone or anything but Jesus. We are to give Jesus first place in our lives (1 Thes. 1:9). We are warned to keep ourselves from idols (1 John 5:21). Jesus deserves our love, worship, attention and utmost respect (Deut.6:5). The scripture declares that the Word of the Lord came to Ezekiel to tell him that men had set up idols in their hearts and that they had put stumbling-blocks before their faces. The Lord warned them that they should repent, turn from their idols and renounce their detestable practices. (See Ezekiel 14) *We are special people with special blessings on our lives and we should value who we are, who we belong to and serve Him only* (1 Peter 2:9-12 NIV).

Jealousy: Jealousy is the feeling of anger or bitterness of someone who thinks that they should have the qualities or possessions that another person has. We are encouraged to keep away from all jealousy and to clothe ourselves with the Lord Jesus Christ (Romans 13:13-14). We should not be jealous of anyone's achievements or their talents or their skills or their family. We are to wish each other well and always pray for each other. We should not limit God's greatness, because the same God who provides for our brothers and sisters is more than able to do the same for us. Jealousy is dangerous and it is not spiritually fruitful. Whoever operates in jealousy is abusive and limited, and such people also encourage disorder. (See Acts 13:44).

Whenever we become jealous, we are refusing to see our blessings and the favour that the Lord has given to us. We are also not tapping into the vast resources that the Lord has given to all of us. (See Luke 15:11-32) God is well able to do great things in our lives. He loves and cares for all His children. When we trust Him, He will turn up with our blessings just at the right time.

Killing: Killing is the deliberate act of killing someone or an animal. We have to be willing to say 'no' to killing. Taking a life is cruel and hurtful to others. The scripture warns us **NOT** to kill. (See Exodus 20:13)

Malice: Malice is behaviour that is intended to harm others. Malice should not be encouraged. Malice makes us unclean. (See Mark 7:21) We are to follow the ways of God and abide in His Word. If we refuse to follow God's Word and to put it into practice, we will be filled with all kinds of wickedness, including malice. (See Romans 2:29)

Rebellion: Rebellion can be viewed as violent action organised by a large group of people. Rebellion is not welcomed in God's plan and those who rebel will not be successful in the plans of God. *It is only an evil man who is bent on rebellion. And a merciless official will be sent against him* (Proverbs 17:11).

Slander: Slander is to speak untruthful words about another with the intention of damaging their reputation. We are to protect each other's reputation and do not say things about each other which we are not sure of. The scripture says that we are not to slander anyone, but be peaceable and considerate and to show humility to all (Titus 3:2). Whenever we slander others, we cause grief. (2 Corinthians 12:21). He wants us to increase in every area of our life. *Those who speak maliciously and slander others will be ashamed* (1 Peter 3:16). *Whenever we slander our brothers and sisters, we speak against God's law* (James 4:11).

Stinginess: If you describe someone as stingy, you are criticising them for being unwilling to spend money. We should avoid stinginess. Stinginess can prevent us from excelling. We are warned not to eat the food of those who are stingy. (See Proverbs 23:6) *Stinginess keeps us in poverty* (Proverbs 28:22). The Song writer says we are to give and it will come back to us. We will not lose out when we give to those who are in need. We are to be kind and generous with our money, our clothes, our food, our time and with our words. Kind words will cheer each other up, so let's be generous. *If a man shuts his ears from the cry of the poor, he, too, will cry out and will not be answered* (Proverbs 21:13).

Ungodliness: Someone who is morally bad or opposed to religion is described as being ungodly. The scripture also talks about ungodliness, and those who practise ungodliness are described as fools. (See Isaiah 32) The false prophets of Israel were warned that they would eat bitter food because of their ungodliness. (See Jeremiah 23:15) We are recommended to stay away from ungodly behaviour and serve the Lord only. The grace of God which brings us salvation teaches us to say 'no' to ungodliness. We are encouraged to live upright and godly lives (Titus 2:15).

Violence: Violence is behaviour which is intended to hurt, injure or kill people. The scripture speaks against violence. Violence is behaviour that we should avoid. It is important to recognised that evil is associated with violence. (See Proverbs 4:14-17). Those who are violent will also set out to hurt God's people. (See Acts 21:35)

Witchcraft: Witchcraft is the use of magic powers, especially evil ones. We should not practise witchcraft, because it is a sin. *There can be no peace where witchcraft is practised* (1 Kings 9:22). We are to live by the Spirit of God and avoid witchcraft at all costs. (See Galatians 5:16-20)

The attitudes above are some of the sinful ways and actions that the Lord warns us to reject. In order for us to be able to progress, we have to say 'No' to these attitudes and 'Yes' to God's plans and purposes. The scripture tells us:

> *Since, then, you have been raised with Christ, set your hearts on things above where Christ is seated at the right hand of God. Set your minds on things above, not on earthly things. For you He died, and your life is now hidden with Christ in God. When Christ, who is your life, appears, then you will appear with Him in glory. Put to death, therefore, whatever belongs to your earthly nature: sexual immorality, impurity, lust, evil desires and greed, which is idolatry.*

> (Colossians 3:1-5 NIV)

David asked the Lord to keep him from sin and not to allow it to rule his life. These principles apply to all of us today. (See Psalm 19:13-14 NIV) We have to devote ourselves to doing what is good and not allow sin to rule our lives.

There are all types of sinful actions taking place in our world today, but we are encouraged to say 'no' to them.

HOW DID JESUS DEAL WITH THOSE WHO SINNED?

While Jesus was here on Earth, He was also living in a world where people were committing all kinds of sins. But Jesus did not sin and He used different methods to deal with sinful issues. He taught His disciples how to deal with sinners (Matthew 7:14). Jesus went where sinners were and spoke with them (Luke 15:1-6). He told His disciples that there were many things that would come that would cause people to sin (Luke 17:1-5). He forgave sinners (John:8). He restored sinners and told them to leave their lives of sin (John 8:11). Jesus showed love, compassion, forgiveness and He also left us many great examples to follow.

Jesus did many things when dealing with sin and sinners while He was here. What He did was useful for us because we can learn from His examples. There is a great instance in the Bible where Jesus forgave a woman who was taken in adultery. The scripture says that the teachers of the law and the Pharisees brought her to Jesus, suggesting that she should be stoned. But Jesus did not encourage their actions. He spoke to their consciences and challenged them to take action if they had no sin (John 8:7b). But none of them could cast a stone according to the standard by which they had judged the woman. If we ask why they could not cast a stone, then we can see that they all had done things in their lives which also required then to be stoned. None of us should be too quick to condemn others, because we all done things which should be forgiven.

Jesus forgave her and told her to leave her sinful life. All her accusers had to leave her alone because none of them was without sin. This woman was left ALONE with Jesus. This is a perfect place to be. ALONE WITH JESUS! We can always go to Jesus with our worst sins and failures and always be alone with Him, because He will not turn His back on us and He will not speak of our faults to anyone. He wants us to acknowledge Him in all our ways and to turn to Him. When we take every situation to Him, He will always console, support, restore and pardon us. WE SERVE AN AWSOME GOD! There is no condemnation of those who are following Him. He did not condemn the woman. He will not condemn any of us, whenever we acknowledge our sins and go to Him. He will instead give us hope and a new life. All Jesus wants us to do is to say 'NO' TO SIN! *"Then neither do I condemn you", Jesus declared. "Go now, and leave your life of sin."* (John 8:11 NIV)

Jesus did not condemn her. Rather, He encouraged her to turn away from sinful ways and then He forgave her. The same thing that Jesus wanted for this woman is the same thing that He also wants from us.

Jesus also set us a great example when He met Zacchaeus. Zacchaeus was a sinner and a tax collector. Jesus told Zacchaeus that he should come down out of the tree, because He wanted to bring salvation to his home. When Jesus stayed with Zacchaeus, Zacchaeus' attitude changed and he was able to identify his faults. He even offered to return money to the people whom he had cheated before he gave his life to Jesus. We could see that Zacchaeus was immediately convicted of his sins when he met Jesus. Jesus knew how to deal with sinners without condemning them. When Jesus is with sinners they are convicted and they want to get rid of all their sinful ways. This then leads them to repent and then to follow Him. Zacchaeus received salvation because Jesus was with him and in Jesus's presence he recognised his sins and then fully repented. (See Luke 19:1-9)

When Jesus met the woman at the well, her life was in a total mess. She was confused and lived a morally sinful life which excluded her from her community because of her unacceptable behaviour. He spoke to her in a unique way that allowed her to turn her life around and follow Him. (See John 4:16) Jesus pointed out the area of sin that was most prominent in her life. She could not deny her action, but acknowledged her faults and went to tell others about Jesus. Jesus did not point out her failures and condemn her. He spoke with her and promised her something which was everlasting and life-changing. (See John 4:10). He revealed Himself to her in a magnificent way. Christ's action transformed her life and helped her to become a dynamic preacher and evangelist. Many came to accept the Lord because of her words (John 4:39-42). Her simple message was: Come and see a man who has told her all the things that ever she did. Is He not the Christ?

Jesus extended forgiveness to people who attacked Him personally. This happened in Samaria when many people rejected Him, mocked Him and treated Him badly. But He did not retaliate. The disciples wanted to call down fire from heaven to destroy these people, but He rebuked them and told them, that He did not come to destroy but to save. (See Luke 9:51-56). Jesus's action was remarkable in all areas. Where sin had caused brokenness, fear and exclusion, Jesus made full restoration. He came to save. He came to forgive and to allow us to have new life in Him. *He is the Lamb of God who takes away the sin of the world* (John 1:29). He wants us to follow Him and to say 'no' to sin.

HOW SHOULD WE DEAL WITH OTHERS WHO SIN AND WITH OUR OWN SINFUL ATTITUDES?

Jesus left many great examples for us to follow. He taught us how to treat our brothers and sisters. He taught us how to forgive, how to listen, how to make restoration and also to encourage others. (See Matthew 18:15-18). Daily, we are to learn to be like Jesus. We also have to learn to forgive one another and work with each other, no matter what others may have done. We are not excluded from what Jesus said to Peter when he told him about the number of times he should forgive his brother. (See Matthew 18:22) Jesus our Saviour forgave many of us many, many times. The scripture declares that we are to forgive each other, just as Christ forgave us (Matthews 6:14-15).

There are times when we can be hurt by others, both believers and non-believers. But we have to learn to forgive and to carry on with each other.

Here is an example of Steven, a great man of God, who was beaten and stoned to death, not because he had done anything wicked, but because he loved and talked about the Lord. Yet, when they were stoning him, he did not curse them, but he asked the Lord NOT to hold their sins against them (Acts 7:60). He forgave them even when they were killing him. This is a sincere and genuine display of total forgiveness! We all have to learn to forgive others who hurt us cruelly.

It is also important that we be careful not to judge or condemn others whenever they fall into sin. Often we pay attention to other people's faults and judge them, but we are to look at our own faults before we judge others. We should be quick to show compassion and mercy. **Let's look at what this scripture says:** *Why do you look at the speck of sawdust in your brother's eye and pay no attention to the plank in* *your own eye? How can you say to your brother, Let me take the speck out of your eye? When all the time there is a plank in your eye? You hypocrite, first take the plank out of your own eye, and then you will see clearly to remove the speck from your brother's eye* (Matthew 7:3-5 NIV) We should not judge or condemn each other. WHY? Because *we will all stand before God's judgement seat* (Romans 14:10). *We are to suffer with each other* (Colossians 3:13).

Many individuals fall into sin and instead of asking for forgiveness and returning to the Lord, they choose to go deeper into sin. We are to encourage them to turn away from their sins and repent. There are severe consequences when individuals choose to constantly keep falling deeper and deeper into sin. For example, in the Book of Genesis, Chapter 3, Adam and Eve disobeyed the Lord. And by Chapter 4, Cain murdered his brother, Abel. In Chapter 6, sin was so rampant that the Lord repented that he made humanity. This resulted in God's judgment when He sent The Flood.

We are to be examples in all our ways by helping others to be victorious over-comers. Many of the qualities are outlined in the scripture that we are to apply in our lives in order to please the Lord and to win the respect of others. (See 1 Thessalonians 4:1-11)

We are to be careful not use our tongues, to gossip, put others down, exaggerate, complain or manipulate others. Our actions should demonstrate that Jesus lives, reigns and rules in us. It is crucial that we depend on the Holy Spirit to give us the strength to say 'No' to all the destruction that the tongue can cause. (See James:3) People may come to us and confess their faults. We are required to be mature Christians and maintain confidentiality. We should not condemn anyone, but aim to build confidence and self-esteem. Our responsibility is to be like Jesus by asking Him for the wisdom that does not condemn others. We must be careful not to speak any negative words against anyone, including our brothers. *Anyone who speaks against his brother or judges him speaks against the Law and judges it* (James 4:11). If you are reading this book and you have used your tongue to cause any grief in the past, please ask the Lord to forgive you.

We also have to learn to forgive ourselves as believers. God does not condemn us and our standing before Him remains the same. Whenever we make mistakes we have to ask Him to forgive us because Jesus already paid the price for our sins on the cross. (See 1 Corinthians 15:3) We have to learn to forgive ourselves for our past sins and not to keep ourselves in bondage. The Lord is merciful and is always willing to forgive His people. He is forgiving and restoring from the beginning. For example, Adam and Eve were expelled from the Garden of Eden for their disobedience, but the Lord clothed them. (See Genesis:3) Cain killed his brother and became a wanderer, but the Lord gave him a mark of protection (Genesis 4:15). The flood came and destroyed the people, but Noah and his family were saved (Genesis:7).

Regardless of what we have done in the past, Jesus has forgiven us and we are to move on. *So if the Son sets you free, you will be free indeed* (John 8:36). We are members of His family. We are to say sorry to Him, sorry to others and continue to serve the Lord. Confess to others and keep on serving the Lord.

> *If we confess our sins, he is faithful and just and will forgive us our sins and purify us from all unrighteousness* (1 John 1:9 NIV).

We should also declare God's Word over the wrong things we have done by meditating on His Word and speaking to ourselves. Continue telling yourself that you are a child of God, you are an over-comer and you will not do that sinful action again. Tell yourself that you won't be a slave any longer to sin. (See John 8:34)

Over the years I struggled with many issues in my life and I also made some mistakes. At those times I had to call upon the Lord Jesus many times to forgive me. Many of the things that I did in the past the Lord has helped me to overcome them, so much so that I can look at them now and sincerely thank the Lord that I do not do those things again! Jesus is still helping me to say 'No' to those things each time that they come around. He can do the same for all of us. Whatever you are struggling with, be brave and say **NO** to sin. The

Lord wants us to overcome our weaknesses. He also wants us to be truthful and honest and to live a successful Christian life.

I have also seen many believers who have made mistakes and have asked the Lord for forgiveness and they have now gone on to do great works for the Lord. This is not the time to give up. Keep loving and serving the Lord with all your heart. My encouragement to you is not to return to doing the things that you used to do before you gave your heart and life to Jesus. If you do make any further mistakes, always come back to JESUS and ask Him to forgive you. Jesus is faithful and He will never leave you or forsake you or let you down. It does not matter what you have done, He will forgive you as long as you truly repent and turn away from the sin that breaks His heart! *We all have sinned and fall short of the glory of God* (Romans 3:23). But Jesus loves us so much He is always willing to forgive us and to give us a second chance.

Many individuals in the Bible made mistakes and they had to deal with the consequences of their mistakes. They confessed, repented, asked the Lord to forgive them, and then they continued serving Him. We cannot hide from God because He sees all our mistakes and failures. Our responsibility is simply to ask Him to forgive us. The scripture verse says:

> *Therefore, since we have a great high priest who has gone through the heavens, Jesus the Son of God, let us hold firmly to the faith we profess. For we do not have a high priest who is unable to sympathise with our weakness, but we have one who has been tempted in every way, just as we are, yet was without sin. Let us then approach the throne of grace with confidence, so that we may receive mercy and find grace to help us in our time of need.*

> (Hebrews 4:14-16 NIV)

King David is a perfect example of someone who kept making mistakes However, he always returned to the Lord and asked for forgiveness. (See 2 Samuel 12) The Lord had mercy on him and forgave him for the evil that he had done. David acknowledged his sin before the Lord and poured out his heart unto God. (See Psalm 51:1-4) This is what the Lord wants us to do, to turn to Him and repent.

The apostle Paul encourages the Christian believer to fight a good fight, keep the faith and finish the course. And in so doing, they will be rewarded with a crown of righteousness. (See 2 Timothy 4:7)

Paul also mentioned his struggle with sin. He testified that it was his sincere desire to do good, but evil always presented itself. The presence of evil was the cause of his failure to do the good that he wanted to do. He stated that he continued to do the things that he did not want to do. Paul mentions how he could see another law working in his body and trying to make him a prisoner to sin, but in spite of all the struggles, Paul gave thanks to Jesus who rescued him from sin. (See Romans 7)

Being a believer in Christ does not exempt us from being tempted to sin. We are encouraged to be on our guard and avoid the plans of the enemy. Jesus conquered sin once and for all, and he will fight by our side if we look to Him for help.

To help us be strong, reading his Word and then confess it over our lives.

Jesus himself was tempted, but He never sinned. (See Hebrews 4:15) We are to put our trust in Him. Because he himself suffered when he was tempted, he is able to help those who are being tempted (Hebrews 2:18 NIV). He said that He will not allow us to be tempted more than we are able to endure. (See 1 Corinthians 10:13) Jesus sent the enemy flying by using the Word when He was tempted. (See Matthew 4:4-10) We can do the same damage to the enemy's plan whenever we use this powerful tool, The Word! *We can resist all temptation* (Ephesians 6:10-19).

THE PUNISHMENT FOR SINS:

There are always penalties for our sins. Whenever we refuse to follow God's commands, there will always be some consequence. (See Numbers 5:31) *Sin displeases the Father* (Ephesians 4:30). We read that Adam and Eve, the first two people who disobeyed God's command, received a penalty for their sins. They were embarrassed, they became fearful, and then they were expelled from the Garden of Eden. (See Genesis:3)

Whenever we sin, the Lord's wrath is poured out upon us. *He loves us but sin disciplines Him, because He is righteous* (Hebrews 12:6). Our sinful actions result in guilt. He is not complacent when it comes to sin. He always judges and acts against sin. Our sinful acts affect our progress, our family, our relationship with the Lord and our friends. The Bible says: *The wrath of God is being revealed from heaven against all the godlessness and wickedness of men who suppress the truth by their wickedness* (Romans 1:18).

Our Lord delights in righteousness (Jeremiah 9:24).

Don't you know that when you offer yourselves to something to obey him as slaves, you are slaves to the one whom you obey, whether you are slaves to sin, which leads to death, or to obedience, which leads to righteousness.

(Romans 6:16-17)

The Lord told the children of Israel that they would have to bear the consequences of their detestable practices. He warned them that He would deal with them as they deserved. He informed them that they would be ashamed and they would not be able to open their mouths because of their actions (Ezekiel 16:58-63). *Our sins will also find us out* (Numbers 32:23 NIV).

Our sins also hurt others. The Book of Joshua shows us how The Lord commanded the children of Israel that they should not take any of the devoted things from Ai. But Achan disobeyed the Lord's command and, because of his disobedient action, the children of Israel were defeated in battle (Joshua 7). His action caused the loss of thirty-six lives. (See Joshua 7:6). Achan's action affected his family, all of whom were killed.

> Then Joshua, together with all Israel, took Achan, son of Zerah, the silver, the robe, the gold wedge, his sons and daughters, his cattle, donkeys and sheep, his tent and all that he had to the Valley of Anchor. Joshua said, "Why have you brought this trouble on us? The Lord will bring trouble on you today." Then all Israel stoned him.

(Joshua 7:24-25).

Achan's children and his livestock were destroyed because of his disobedience. There is a penalty for our sinful actions and it does not only affect us, but also hurts others. Because of this we need to be careful of the things that we do and say. Often times when we fall into sin, we also damage our church's reputation and our friends. Sin causes hurt, rejection, exclusion, embarrassment and death. Let us all think before we disobey any of the Lord's commands. *The soul who sins is the one who will die* (Ezekiel 18:4 (NIV). *Greater is the one in us than the one in the world.* (See 1 John 4:4)

Sometimes disciplinary measures are carried out in our churches when believers continue to commit sin and make no effort to change. For example, people are excluded from office, asked to step down from certain positions and some individuals are required to apologise, while some have been taken to other ministers to be disciplined. These actions to correct church failures can be avoided if we are willing and SAY 'NO' TO SIN.

The Book of Corinthians took note when some believers sinned. (See 1 Corinthians:5) The scripture verse said: *Those who sin are to be rebuked publicly, so that the others my take warning* (1 Timothy 5:20). The devil has a way to show us things that are false, yet he lets them appear real. His plan is to steal our joy and all our successes. Be aware and say 'no' to all forms of ungodliness. We are not to listen to any of his lies and disobey God's laws. Our aim as God's children is to become like Christ, which is a lifelong process. Do not allow the ways of the world to domineer your life. *Do not gratify the cravings of the sinful nature* (Ephesians 2:1-5).

> *Stand firm then, with the belt of truth buckled round your waist, with the breastplate of righteousness in place, and with your feet fitted with the readiness that comes from the gospel of peace. In addition to this, take up the shield of faith, with which you can extinguish all the flaming arrows of the evil one. Take the helmet of salvation and sword of the Spirit, which is the word of God. And pray in the Spirit and all occasions with all kinds of prayers and requests. With this in mind, be alert and always keep on praying for all the saints.*

(Ephesians 6:13-18 NIV)

This chapter outlines some of the sinful actions that we can be involved in and how Jesus dealt with sin. It also makes mention of the best ways to say 'no' to sin and to follow Jesus with a clean hand and a pure heart, as Jesus knows all about us and He wants us to follow His ways. So let us say 'NO' TO ALL KINDS OF SINS: 'no' to **a**nger, to **b**ackbiting, to **c**ovetousness, to **d**isobedience, to **e**nvy, to **f**ilthy language, to **g**reed, to **h**atred, to **i**njustice, to **j**ealousy, to **k**illing, to **l**ying, 'no' to **m**alice, to **n**egative words, to **o**ppression, to **p**utting others down, to **q**uarrelling, to **r**ebellion, to **s**exual immorality, to **t**emptations, to **u**nforgiveness, to **v**iolence, to **w**itchcraft and 'no' to a sinful **y**oke.

Let's fight the good fight of faith and hold on to God's Word because His Word gives life and it bring changes.

LET'S SAY 'NO' TO SIN AND LIVE A SUCCESSFUL CHRISTIAN LIFE FOR THE KING.

Chapter Seven

BE WILLING TO SERVE AND LEAD OTHERS WELL

The Lord has made all of us and placed us on this earth for a purpose. He has given us abilities, skills and talents to serve Him and others and to make a difference. None of us was given all these outstanding gifts to lie dormant; we were given them to use to serve the Lord and others. One of the best ways we can utilise our abilities is to use them to serve in His house.

The Bible is filled with examples, of how important it is to serve the Lord first with our best skills and talents. In the Book of Haggai we are shown how important it is to give the Lord priority. It tells how the people started to build a temple and were enthusiastic. But after a while they became discouraged and disheartened by their enemies (Haggai 1:1-3) so they stopped working on the temple and started to concentrate on their own houses. Their actions displeased the Lord immensely, and He stopped their blessings.

> *"Why?" declares the Lord Almighty. Because of my house, which remains a ruin, while each of you is busy with his own house? Therefore, because of you, the heavens have withheld their dews and the earth its crops. I called for a drought on the fields and mountains, on the grains, the new wine, the oil and whatever the ground produces, on men and cattle, and on the labour of your hand."*

(Haggai 1:9-10)

The Lord was displeased with the people, and later sent the prophet Haggai to warn them to return to what they were doing and to let them know that they were to put Him first and not to focus on themselves. The people listened to Haggai and resumed building the Lord's house and their whole life was changed. They then started to experience God's riches and blessings once again. (See Haggai 1 and Haggai 2) The Lord wants us all to serve in Him in various ways, with all our skills. He wants us to use the many talents, skills and abilities to build His kingdom here on Earth. This chapter will look at the many ways Jesus served, the attitudes we should display as we serve and the many ministries in our churches that we can serve in.

Jesus our Lord has left us many examples of how to serve. While He was here on Earth, He took time to serve others graciously, in love, with compassion, faithfully, sincerely and with a humble heart. He showed us that serving others should be done to the best of our ability. He served everyone who came in contact with Him without acting superior or inferior, and He served in many areas. Jesus served by:

- washing the disciples' feet
- telling them about the kingdom
- having prayer meetings
- taking time to listen to others' needs
- feeding others
- comforting people
- building people emotionally, spiritually and socially
- healing people
- delivering people
- raising people from the dead

Jesus served in many, many areas recorded all over in the scriptures. He said that He did not come to **be** served, but to serve (Matthew 20:28).

The Bible also records how other believers served wholeheartedly. The apostle Paul served in various capacities. (See Acts 13-27) He also mentions that we are to serve in love: *You, my brother, were called to be free. But do not use your freedom to indulge the sinful nature; rather, serve one another in love* (Galatians 5:13 NIV).

We also read of Mary, how she served Jesus in a magnificent way. The scripture tells that she bought a very expensive perfume and poured it on Jesus' feet and wiped His feet with her hair. (See John 12:3-9)

This is a beautiful, touching way to serve. It is important that we all make an effort to touch the Lord and others in the way we serve. We are to aim to give our best in all that we do.

Despite what others may say or do to us, we are to strive to give our best. While Mary was doing her best, others grumbled and criticized her, and were concerned about the price she paid for the perfume. But Jesus showed that He appreciated her gift and service dearly. The scripture tells us that whatever we do, we are to do it with all our heart, as we work for the Lord and not for men (Colossians 3:23). Whatever skills that He has given us, we are to use them to serve His purposes. Many times we are asked to serve and we often make all kinds of excuses and we also look at our weaknesses. But God wants to use us just the way we are. In spite of our physical, emotional, intellectual and spiritual imperfections, which we all have, He still wants to use us to do extraordinary work.

I have heard people make all kinds of excuses over the years. Some have said:

- They are not holy enough.
- God can never use them.
- They are not clever enough.
- They have not got enough time.
- They have not known the Lord long enough.

And many more excuses. Nonetheless, I have seen God use many of these people to do tremendous work after they start surrendering to Him. Many have gone on to become leaders, pastors, and teachers and to do many other excellent tasks. It has happened time and time again. Both in the Bible and in this present generation, people have always made excuses. Nonetheless, we are all able to do what the Lord calls us to do, in spite of our excuses, faults, weaknesses and what others say or think about us or even what we may think about ourselves. God made us and He is the one who has placed all these gifts inside of us and He wants us to use them for His purposes. He knew us before we were born. *Before I formed you in the womb I knew you, before you were born I set you apart; I appointed you a prophet to the nations* (Jeremiah 1:5).

The Psalmist also declared: *Your eyes saw my unformed body. All the days ordained for me were written in your book before one of them came to be* (Psalms 139:16).

God has already decided the role that He wants us to play on this Earth. He has already fashioned us for the task. Therefore, whatever He calls you to do, you are to take heart and serve His purposes.

The Bible is filled with examples of believers making excuses. When the Lord called Moses and Gideon, they both came up with good excuses. Moses said that he could not speak (Exodus 4:10). And Gideon said that his family was too weak for him to become a leader (Judges 6:15). Nonetheless, both these men went on to lead, comfort, and create dynamic changes in their generation. God can use any of us to do great things. *We are God's workmanship created in Christ Jesus to do good works, which God prepared in advance for us to do* (Ephesians 2:10). He is always using ordinary people to do extraordinary work and all we need to do is to surrender all our unpleasant attitudes, weaknesses, and past failures and allow Him to use us to do magnificent work.

ATTITUDE AS WE SERVE

As we serve it is important that we all aim to exercise good qualities. The following are some of the attitudes we can display:

- Do not compare yourselves with others. (See Galatians 6:4)
- Celebrate what God has given us.

- Use what you have for His glory. His Word says: *However, He has given each one of us special gifts according to the generosity of Christ* (Ephesians 4:7 NIV).

We should be aware that we are not called to do everything. Jesus wants and loves us just the way we are. All of us have limitations and weaknesses and we make mistakes. But He is able to hide all our sins (see Psalms 103:12) and to use us as if we have never made any mistake.

Remember to be positive, keep focused, look to Jesus and serve Him to the best of your ability. Our behaviour should demonstrate to others the love of Christ. As we serve, let us also aim to pay attention to the needs of others, love and exalt Jesus. Honour Christ and others. The scripture says we are to serve wholeheartedly (Ephesians 6:7-8). Jesus also said that we are to be careful not to do our acts of righteousness before men, to be seen by them, because if we do so, we will have no reward from our father in heaven (Matthew 6:1). As we serve, make every effort to:

Be faithful: As we serve, we are to strive be faithful to our ministry. If you are asked to serve in any ministry, it is important that you remain committed! For example, be there on time and prepare for whatever you are asked to do. If you are unable to carry out your duty, remember to let your leader know. You can always phone or send a text messages. People and the Lord are depending on you and Jesus is waiting to say to all of us: "*Well done, good and faithful servant! You have been faithful with a few things; I will put you in charge of many things. Come and share your Master's happiness!*" (Matthew 25:23).

Show respect: We should show respect as we serve, both to our leaders and to others. It is important that we speak to each other respectfully, listen attentively, create friendship, and encourage each other and:

Offer hospitality to one another without grumbling. Each one should use whatever gifts he has received to serve others, faithfully administering God's grace in its various forms in unity, cheerfully and enthusiastically.

(1 Peter 4:9 10)

None of us is an island. We all need each other, and the scripture says we are to: *Carry each other's burdens, and in this way you will fulfil the law of Christ* (Galatians 6:2). It is also crucial that we appreciate each others' gifts and abilities and always give compliments to each other.

Give support: It is advisable to support each others' efforts. Please remember to give compliments, to say thank you, to give good advice and always help others to improve in their work. We should not envy each other, but always do our best to encourage.

The scripture says: *Let us not become conceited, provoking and envying each other.* (Galatians 5:26)

> *Each one should test his own actions. Then he can take pride in himself, without comparing himself to somebody else, for each one should carry his own load* (Galatians 6:4-5)

We can do all things through Christ who strengthens us. So let us offer our bodies as living sacrifices to God as the scripture states:

> *Therefore, I urge you, brothers, in view of God's mercy, to offer your bodies as living sacrifices to God. This is your spiritual act of worship. Do not conform any longer to the pattern of this world, but be transformed by the renewing of your mind. Then you will be able to test and approve what God's will is his good pleasing and perfect will. For by the grace given me, I say to every one of you: do not think of yourself more highly than you ought, but rather think of yourself with sober judgement, in accordance with the measure of faith God has given you.*

(Romans 12:1-3 NIV)

Be patient: As we serve it is also important that we learn to be patient with others. Although we are all made in His own image and likeness, nevertheless, we are all different. Many of us are from different backgrounds, with different experiences and we do things differently. Some of us will take longer to do certain tasks, and to change and learn. Nevertheless, we are to be patient with each other. God is patient with us, so let's be patient with others. (See Peter 3:9) *A patient man also has great understanding* (Proverbs 14:29).

Humility: As we serve, it is important that we humble ourselves in His service. The Lord is expecting us to be modest as we serve. Jesus was a great example. He did many menial tasks. He washed the disciples' feet, fed the hungry and comforted the depressed and lonely. His Word also declared: *I have set you an example that you should do as I have done for you* (John 13:15). The scripture also says: *Be completely humble and gentle; be patient, bearing with one another in love* (Ephesians 4:2 NIV).

Keep learning: As we serve, it is also wise for us to keep learning. Learn from others, learn from books and learn by doing courses. The wise will store up knowledge. (See Proverbs 10:14)

The Bible tells us that we were made to rule over all the Earth. We are also commanded to be fruitful, to increase in number, to subdue and to rule over everything that moves. (See Genesis 1:26-26) But there are times when we will be required to do menial tasks, sometimes practical tasks and sometimes we may have to serve in unfamiliar areas and are required to do things that are quite daunting. But we are to speak to the Lord during these times about these situations and be willing to learn and share ideas. Many times the Lord will allow us to be in these places because He wants to build us up, to prune us so that we can be stronger and give better service. God will move us to different areas whenever it is appropriate. We should never think that He has forgotten us. Let us do as Paul says, to give ourselves fully to the work of the Lord (1 Corinthians 15:58).

If you are a new Christian, there are many ministries in our churches that you can serve in.

It is important that you start doing something as soon as possible and whatever you choose to do will be highly appreciated. You can speak to someone in the church and let them know that you would like to do something. You should also pray and tell the Lord about your desire. Ask Him to direct you into the right area of service. God knows all about you. He know all that He placed inside of you and He is willing to reveal your potential and skills if you ask Him to.

There are also times when we will be appointed to some ministries by leaders or ministers or by older members. But there are times when we can also take the initiative and start doing something. There is lots of work to be done in our churches and in our communities and in other countries.

When Jesus appointed the seventy-two, He told them that there was lots of work to be done, but there were few people to do it, and they were to pray and ask the Lord to send more workers (Luke 10:1-3). And even today we can still say that there is much to be done. For example, at Mount Zion where I worship, there is still plenty of work to be done. Some of the areas you can serve in are:

Administration: If you are able to do administration, many churches are willing to accept people in this area of duty. Your church will inform you of the duties that they require. At most churches you will be asked to assist in the church office, to answer the phone, help with filing, computing and other office tasks.

You are expected to be committed, trustworthy, understanding, confidential and be willing to work as a team and be supportive.

All churches will be able to train and support you. Your talents and skills in this area will be highly appreciated.

Sunday School: Serving in the Sunday School department is a challenging task, but you will be welcome in this department. You will always be supported by the Sunday School leaders and staff.

You will be asked to complete a form (CRB in England)) by the Sunday School department, for child protection purposes. Sunday School duties involve teaching the children to serve God in their generation and to be young disciples and leaders to their peers. You will also teach the children Bible stories, songs, assist with behaviour management, accompany them on outings, and speak to parents and carers.

Helpers should always aim to meet the children's learning needs and ensure that they are in a safe environment. Helpers should be willing to learn, especially Bibles stories, be enthusiastic, committed, good role models, determined, patient, tolerant, honest and gentle. Sunday School workers are expected to build self-confidence in the children and to co-operate with parents and others. Being a Sunday School teacher is rewarding as you are always aiming to encourage your students to have high aspirations and to let them know they are unique, blessed, and special and that Jesus loves them.

Ushering: Serving on the ushering team is a fulfilling task. You are the first point of contact on a Sunday morning. An usher should always welcome people warmly, smile, shake hands, and be polite, alert, approachable, friendly and welcoming.

Ushers should be aware of the day's main activities, such as dedications, baptism and the names of the preacher and guest speakers. They have to accompany people to their seats, assist in altar ministries, help to collect the offerings and learn how to deal with difficult people.

New believers are always welcome on the ushering team at most churches; all that is needed is to offer your services. All our churches need vibrant, dedicated and enthusiastic people on their ushering team. You will be offered advice and training before you are assigned to a team. If you are a new believer and are not aware of the ushering activities, you can always speak to a member at your local church or a member of the ushering team. Someone will be happy to assist you.

Cleaning and Catering: Serving on the cleaning and catering teams are physical duties, calling for commitment, dedication and hard work. Your roles are to cook, serve, and clean. Every church needs cleaners, though not all churches provide food on a Sunday as we do at my church. But if your church or a church that you are planning on attending is involved in catering you can ask if it is possible for you to assist with this. At most churches you can contact the church office.

It is our responsibility to keep our building clean and tidy. Cleaning involves taking care of the building, cleaning the toilets, dusting the chairs, cleaning the kitchen, washing dishes, vacuuming and cleaning the doors. If you can offer your service in this area it is always highly valued and appreciated.

Music and worship: The music team plays the musical instruments and those on the worship team sing and worship. If you are gifted at playing the drums, guitar, piano or any other instrument, you can offer your service. If you also desire to serve in this area and are unable to play any of these instruments, you can still be trained. In many of our churches people are always willing to train and nurture people to play an instrument. Speak to someone who leads the worship in the church.

If you are interested in singing and joining the worship team and helping to lead the worship service, you can also speak to someone. It is crucial that as you offer your service in these areas that you take time to pray and to ask the Lord for strength, for wisdom, vision and direction, so that lives can be touched, renewed and come to know the Lord Jesus.

Media team: On the media team you will film the service and assist with the overhead projector. Your service is always welcome in His house and you will receive training and support from members who are responsible for this ministry.

Hospitality: Serving on the hospitality team, your duties are to serve refreshments to those who are ministering. You will be required to prepare water for the worship team, the speaker, and all those who are ministering. The hospitality team also caters for visiting preachers and their families. Most churches will welcome new believers to serve on the hospitality team.

Caring team: The caring team are those who take care of the sick and the vulnerable. They visit the sick and offer their services. In most cases they offer prayer, read the Word to them, speak with people in their homes and offer help in areas where they need assistance. If you are willing to assist in this area you can speak with someone in your church. Maybe there isn't a caring team in your church. This is a great opportunity to start setting up a team, to help the needy and older brethren. A caring team is a vital part of ministry.

Youth ministry: In the Youth ministry, there are different activities to perform. There is usually a Youth Pastor or leader who is in charge of the youth department. The Youth Pastor allocates tasks and various activities to the young people. The youths usually meet once per week in most churches, mainly on a Friday evening.

At my church they conduct Bible studies, games, go on trips, go out for lunch and drinks, attend youth conferences and form good, friendly relationships. It is a dynamic ministry and all young believers should try to find out more about this ministry and attend. Parents and careers will find it a wonderful place to get their children involved. Young people will find it interesting and be able to meet friends and also have the opportunity to develop and expose their talents and skills.

Street Pastor: To serve as a Street Pastor, you will have to be a member of a local church. You will receive training in counselling, drug awareness, the way the community works and street safety. You will need to speak to your Pastor or an elder before you can join up as a street pastor. Your duties will be to go on the street and in clubs and pubs and speak to people, tell them about the love of Jesus, show compassion, listen and build hope.

Street pastors have seen remarkable results in the past: a drop in crime, lives transformed and restored. The Word of God says: we are to go to the byways and edges and spread the Good News and this is what our Street Pastors will do and are doing.

Prayer Team: Many churches also have prayer teams. The role of the prayer team is to:

- conduct prayer meetings of many types
- pray with others on the altar
- pray for special prayer requests in the week
- lead special prayer meetings
- pray for the broken, destitute. the discouraged and the sick
- pray for the community and all other needs

You can obtain training, guidance and encouragement from pastors, elders, youth leaders, or other members and leaders. Being a member of the prayer team will help you to grow spiritually and also take you to another level in Christ.

Driver: Many churches need drivers. Drivers drive the church vans and pick up senior members of the church on Sundays. At some churches there are also drivers to collect Sunday School children. You can enquire at the church you attend and find out how to volunteer to become a driver. A driver has to be someone with a clean driver's licence, a willing heart and who is kind, committed and trustworthy.

Drama and Dance Group: The drama and dance groups are always functioning. Their roles are to dance, put on plays and worship God in an awesome fashion. Many of our young people are members of this group; they always put on excellent programmes and lift up the name of Jesus in a lively way. This ministry is **not** limited to young people alone. If you want to join these groups, speak to the leader or phone the church where you attend.

Men's and Women's Ministry: As you become members at your church, you can join the Men's or Women Ministry. They often have various activities such as prayer breakfasts, football and cricket games. They also plan week-end breaks, dancing and special birthday parties.

New Christian Worker: The duties of the New Christian Workers are to speak to new believers, pray with them, encourage them, tell them about the Lord Jesus, take their names and contact details and inform them of church activities and about baptism. The church is always happy to train New Christian Workers.

International worker: There are times when some people may be called to do international ministries. Some may become evangelists or international speakers. There are no limits to what God can do with our lives. God is always willing to lead us into greater pastures. If you are willing to serve abroad, start praying for:

- Other nations
- For the ability to be able to speak to others effectively
- For provision
- For favour and wisdom
- For willingness to do His work.

It is important to start saving and to do short trips abroad. As you prepare to serve, the Lord will enlarge your heart, your vision and deepen your compassion and fill you with joy for service.

Leaders: Many believers will become leaders after they have worked in ministries for a while. You can be asked to become a connect group leader or house group leader, an elder or a pastor, or to lead in any ministries.

If you have been asked to become a leader, it is important that you take time to pray and seek the Lord for wisdom, confidence and favour. It is wise do some courses in management and leadership, to continue to develop your skills and keep putting God first and also not to be afraid to ask others for advice.

As you take on this amazing task, be ready to take charge and to accept changes. In the Book of Acts, there is a great example that I think everyone should follow as they take on a leadership role. In this example, the disciples faced a difficult matter with which they had to deal: conflict between two groups of people. Their only help was to seek the Lord for guidance and wisdom. They had to delegate tasks, organise meetings, pray, confront changes, face challenges and build confidence. These are some of the issues that leaders will have to deal with and we should ALWAYS SEEK THE LORD! (Acts 6:1-7).

There are times when leaders will be faced with all kinds of difficult tasks. But none of us should shy away from difficulties. We are to learn to lean on Jesus, seek God in everything. He is able to steer people into coping and trusting so that they are able to build their characters and fulfil all their purposes.

Paul mentions some of the characteristics that overseers and deacons should have. He said that an overseer must be someone without reproach, the husband of one wife, temperate, self-controlled, respectable, hospitable and able to teach. He also advised that an overseer should not be a drunkard or violent, but be able to manage his home well.

Peter also laid out several characteristic of a good leader:

> *Shepherd of God's flock that is under your care, serving as overseers not because you must, but because you are willing, as God wants you to be; not greedy for money, but eager to serve; not lording it over those entrusted to you, but being an example to the flock. And when the Chief Shepherd appears, you will receive the crown of glory that will never fade away.*

> (1 Peter 5:1-4 NIV)

These are some of the excellent qualities we are to strive to obtain as we lead others. Leaders are also expected to:

Communicate well: Leaders should be able to communicate effectively. Communication should be clear and effective. They should also be polite, prepared, comfortable and be able to listen attentively to people.

Delegate: All leaders should be able to delegate responsibilities to others. No one can do everything. But before you delegate any task, make sure that people are aware of their task, that they are able to do it, and want to do it, and always pray and seek the Lord for good direction and judgement. (See Exodus 18:13-26)

Listen: Leaders should be able to listen to others. People will come to you with all kinds of issues and it is important that you take time to listen. I am sure you won't have the answer for everything, but always show compassion, respect, give kind words, be positive and give others the opportunity to express themselves and remember to always pray for those who come and share.

Be impartial: It is very important that you do not show any favouritism as leaders. Everyone should be treated fairly and there should be no preferences because of race, status, religious background or association. The Bible tells us that we should not show favouritism:

My brothers, as believers in our glorious Lord Jesus Christ, don't show favouritism. Suppose a man comes into your meeting wearing a gold ring and fine clothes, and a poor man in shabby clothes also comes in. If you show special attention to the man wearing fine clothes and say, "Here is a good seat for you," but say to the poor man, "You stand there" or "Sit on the floor by my feet," have you not discriminated among yourselves and become judges with evil thoughts? Listen, my dear brothers: Has not God chosen those who are poor in the eyes of the world to be rich in faith and to inherit the kingdom he promised those who love him?

(James 2:1-5 NIV)

Prioritise: There are many duties to carry out as leaders but leaders have to prioritise their work. Leaders have to make it their priority to read His Word, call upon His name, and exercise faith in Christ. We should also look out for others who are in need first to assist them and always be ready to focus on more important issues.

Planning meetings: Leaders will have to organise meetings. As a leader, you will have to learn to plan, organise and control meetings. For example, if you are appointed as a connect group leader, you will have to prepare the scripture, have your prayer points and topic, think about how to give others the opportunity to share and always pray before and place things in the hand of the Lord.

Empowering others: Leaders will also have to empower others. Some of the ways to empower others are to give team members tasks, compliments, encouragement and information and train those you are leading to become leaders themselves.

Working as a team: People who serve should work as a team. Some of the best ways to work as a team are to learn to plan with others, to be creative, give encouragement, to listen and to pray with others. None of us knows everything; we should be willing to share what we know with others, to trust one another, to thank one another and give kind words.

Be able to handle change: There will always be changes in our churches, in ministry, in people and in society. We will all experience changes. Change affects every aspect of our lives and we should always be open to changes. It is more productive to follow and lead whenever there are changes. Don't be too quick to resist changes and always seek the Lord before making decisions.

I have been at my church for over sixteen years and I have seen many changes take place. Once, I was even thinking of leaving because of changes. However, after seeking the Lord, I realised that there are changes everywhere and there always will be. God is able to bless and keep us wherever we are. Be patient as believers and leaders when there are changes. We are all able to survive in all kinds of changes because Jesus is with us in all the seasons. Remain positive and trust in God. He will never leave or forsake us. God is the same yesterday, today and forever. Circumstances and situations will change, but His help to comfort, direct and give wisdom never changes. He is always the same.

I have been serving in churches from an early age. I grew up in a church in Jamaica and my grandparents trained me from a child to serve in the church. From a young age, I had to carry sand, water and stone to build the church and did many other activities, which were not easy. But I have seen the Lord work miraculously in my life and in my family's lives. Some of my family are saved and some are preaching the Gospel. He has healed us many times. It is important to train the next generation to serve their purposes and to serve in God's house.

At present I am still serving in my church as I did over the years. I have worked in the Sunday Schools, in Alfa, on the ushering team, on the cleaning team, in hospitality, with street ministry and in other ministries. At the moment I do the hospitality in my church. I find it very rewarding, fulfilling and a pleasure working in God's house. I have also learnt that, whatever I am doing to be committed, willing, hard-working, respect others, speak to others with understanding, have a kind heart and pray and ask the Lord for strength and wisdom. I have heard God speak to me many times while I am serving. He has instructed me, corrected me and promised to bless me. I even heard His voice speak to me and tell me to write this book after serving at my church. I am overwhelmed with the many thanks, compliments and appreciation that I have received from people at my church for my service. They all seem to appreciate my work. Whatever we do, we are to depend on the Lord for strength and guidance.

There are many brothers and sisters at my church who are serving tirelessly. They are faithful, committed, happy, serving the Lord, and display great examples for others to follow, as we should all aim to do and say, like Paul,

> *Never be lacking in zeal, but keep your spiritual favour, serving the Lord. Be joyful in hope, patient in affection, and faithful in prayer. Share with God's people who are in need. Practise hospitality.*

> (Galatians 12:11-13 NIV)

Often times we are so crowded with all kinds of tasks, in our lives: families, work situations, friends and all kinds of issues. These and many other activities can prevent us from serving wholeheartedly and sometimes, too, we are discouraged and put down by others, which can also prevent us from serving. But the Lord wants us to give Him priority and our best always. Many of us have talents and skills that we have not yet utilised. He is waiting for us to start showing off those great skills in His service. It is imperative that we use those skills to fulfil His purposes here on earth. And we should never allow anyone or anything to prevent us from using them for the Lord.

The apostle Paul, writing to Colossians, said: *Whatever you do, work at it with all your heart, as working for the Lord, not for men, since you know that you will receive an inheritance from the Lord as a reward. It is the Lord Christ you are serving* (Col. 3:23-24).

The Bible tells us that we are not to become weary in doing well, for at the proper time we will reap a harvest if we do not give up (Galatians 6:9). God also promised to reward us. He will not withhold His blessings from us. But He will always reward us for all that we have done and are doing. He has all good gifts. (See Isaiah 40:10) He has encouraged us to rejoice and be glad because our rewards will be great and His Father will honour those who serve Him.

> *Whoever serves me must follow me; and where I am, my servant also will be. My Father will honour the one who serves me* (John 12:26 NIV).

142

This chapter has outlined the many areas in which we can serve and lead in our churches. We are encouraged to serve willingly, with a good attitude, faithfully and to be committed. We should also continue to learn and achieve and build others and ourselves as we serve. It has shown the many ministries and duties we can serve in and build God's kingdom here on Earth.

So let us continue to serve as: an **a**postle, as a **b**ishop, serve as **c**aretaker, as a **d**eacon, as an **e**vangelist, without **f**ear, as a **g**ate keeper, as **h**ouse-keeper, as an **i**nstructor, as a **j**anitor, serve with a **k**ind heart, as a **l**eader, as a **m**issionary, serve when it's **n**eeded, serve as an **o**verseer, as a **p**astor, with good **q**ualities, as a **r**apper, as a **S**unday school teacher, as a **t**eacher, as an **u**sher, as a **v**oice trainer, as a **w**indow cleaner, with e**x**cellence, serve as a **y**outh worker, and serve with **z**eal. Let's serve the King of Kings and build His kingdom here on earth. Amen!

Chapter Eight

LEARN TO PROPHESY OVER YOUR LIFE AND IN OTHER PEOPLE'S LIVES

Prophecy can be defined as the method used to communicate future events. During Old Testament times, the prophets received their messages from the Lord, then communicated it to the kings, priests and to ordinary people. They brought words to comfort, strengthen and encourage. They also rebuked wrong-doings, challenged the political system, and spoke out against injustice and oppression. Their actions were able to transform lives, remove barriers, reveal sins and save many lives.

The scripture tells us of the extraordinary prophetic work that men and women did in biblical days. They spoke both to the leaders and to ordinary people. For example, Elisha gave military information to the King of Israel which protected them from the Arameans (2 Kings 6:8-15) and Elijah confronted King Ahab, who killed Naboth and took away his vineyard (see 1 Kings 21:17-19) while Nathan the prophet rebuked King David for his actions of adultery and murder (2 Samuel 12).

Many of these prophets experienced frightening situations. We read that Jeremiah was thrown in a cistern (Jeremiah 38). Isaiah was sawn in pieces, while Ezekiel had the task of prophesying in difficult situations.

Then He said to me, "Prophesy to these bones and say to them, "Dry bones, hear the word of the Lord! This is what the Sovereign Lord says to these bones: I will make breath enter you, and you will come to life. So I prophesied as I was commanded. And as I was prophesying there was a noise, a rattling sound, and the bones came together, bones to bones.

(Ezekiel 37:4, 5 &7 NIV)

Nonetheless, the Lord was always with the prophets to encourage them. The Lord told Ezekiel not to be afraid, although he would face challenges such as rebellion and harsh words, He would be with him. God also empowered Ezekiel and he was able to prophesy in spite of all the obstacles (Ezekiel 2:6-7). He told Jeremiah that those who put their trust in Him are blessed (Jeremiah 17:7). The Lord was with Isaiah and gave him many revelations and comforting words (Isaiah 5:6-60). God is always with His children, despite the obstacles they may face.

The prophetic work continued in the New Testament. Believers prophesied over situations and believed in the Lord, just as Old Testament believers did. For example, Zechariah prophesied over his son, John (Luke 1:67-79). Anna was a prophetess and lived in the temple (Luke 2:36-38). Jesus also sent out prophets (Matthew 23:34) and He said that He did not come to abolish the Prophets, but to fulfil the Law and the Prophets (Matthew 5:17). Jesus empowers believers with the Holy Spirit, so that they can all prophesy.

But you will receive power when the Holy Spirit comes on you, and you will be my witnesses in Jerusalem, and in all Judea and Samaria, and to the ends of the earth (Acts 1:8).

Jesus was described as Prophet, Priest and King.

As we read of the great prophetic work done by believers in both the Old and New Testaments, the comfort, strength and changes they brought through prophetic utterances in their time, we, too, can take heart and know that we also in this generation have a prophetic role to play. We are expected to speak positive words and encourage, comfort and strengthen ourselves and others.

The Bible tells us that we can all prophesy (1 Corinthians 14:31). And more significantly, we have been given the Holy Spirit (Acts 2:38-39) to aid us to prophesy. The scripture tells us that we have the same capability to do magnificent work, just as those men and women did (James 5:17). Plus, we have life and death in our tongue (Proverbs 18:21). Therefore, we have no excuse not to prophesy. We are to speak positive words in our generation and bring comfort, strength and encouragement to ourselves and to others.

It does not matter what position we may hold in the churches, or where we are coming from, we are all are given the freedom to prophesy. Both men, women and children, have got the magnificent opportunity to prophesy. The Lord promised, that He would pour out His Spirit on all of us, and our sons and daughter will prophesy (Joel 2:28).

For all the above reasons we are to activate this dynamite power that the Lord has given to us and speak prophetic word. This chapter will tell us of the ways we should prophesy, the ethics of prophecy and the benefits of prophecy.

The scripture states that the main reasons we prophesy are to strengthen, encourage and comfort each other (1 Corinthians 14:3). There are many examples in the scripture of prophecies that were given to strengthen, encourage and comfort believers in biblical days. The prophet Isaiah spoke words to strengthen and encourage himself and others:

> *Strengthen the feeble hands, steady the knees that give way; say to those with fearful hearts, "Be strong, do not fear; your God will come, He will come with vengeance; with divine retribution, He will come to save you."*

> (Isaiah 35:3-4).

The apostle Paul sent Timothy to the Thessalonians to speak words to strengthen and encourage other believers' faith (Thessalonians 3:2 NIV). The prophet Haggai also prophesied to the people and encouraged them to start building the temple after they had become discouraged and disheartened and started to concentrate on their own houses. He set out to speak to them and encourage them to start building the Lord's house. These are the words Haggai spoke from the Lord to the people: *Go up into the mountains and bring down timber and build the house, so that I may take pleasure in it and be honoured says the Lord* (Haggai 1:8).

We also read how Elisha spoke prophetic words and comforted his servant who was terrified and felt defeated. The servant was frightened because the city was surrounded by enemies who had come to destroy them. But Elisha was not moved by the situation. He took control of it by speaking transforming words. He spoke these words and comforted himself and his servant. He said to his servant: *"Don't be afraid. Those who are with us are more than those who are with them* (2 Kings 6:16).

We can all learn from these outstanding examples, that whenever there is danger and situations look frightening, we are to take authority and speak words of hope and life to change our circumstances and always remember that life and death are in our tongue. Elisha was able to use The Word and comfort his servant. Words are powerful and we are to speak prophetic words. Whenever we are engulfed by frightening circumstances, our words can break down all barriers and crush all the plans of the enemy. The Lord wants believers to be strengthened, encouraged and to find comfort in Him and, for us to have victory and experience blessings, to practise speaking positive prophetic words.

There are ethics laid out in the scripture that tell us how to prophesy. We are told to prophesy responsibly and to prophesy more than we speak in tongues. To communicate effectively, it is important

- to make it simple, so that people can understand
- to encourage each other

- to show respect to others
- not to confuse ourselves or others

God is not a God of disorder (1 Corinthians 14:29-40). These are the instructions given to us to follow as we prophesy.

If you are a new believer and want to learn more about prophecy, you can always ask your pastor or other believers to explain the work of prophesy to you. You can also continue to learn about the subject by reading your Bible, reading other Christian literatures, and listening to audio and other resources. It is also essential to pray and ask the Lord to develop your confidence and understanding about the works of prophecy. God is more than able to direct you and to reveal greater truths to you: *ask and it will be given to you* (Matthew 7:7). You should listen to the Lord and be consistent as He will always encourage us and direct us.

Although we are to learn about prophecy, none of us will be able to grasp everything about the subject in our lifetime. There will always be something new and we will always have different experiences with the working of prophecy. Believers will operate differently in prophecy. Some people can be loud, while some may prophesy quietly. The Holy Spirit is able to take us into new territories. Some of us may find ourselves prophesying or speaking in different circumstances. For example, some may be led to speak prophetic words to just one person; others may speak to groups of people, whilst some may be asked to prophesy to cities and nations.

There are also times when we may experience some extraordinary prophecy from other believers. Believers can approach us and prophesy about issues in our lives that we have never discussed with them or anyone. Often times they can be so accurate, so encouraging and comforting that you may be surprised at the accuracy of their word. Prophecy is able to bring extraordinary relief, hope, joy and comfort to us that we are not able to explain to anyone. God's mighty works are beyond all we are able to fathom. Let us continue to learn about prophecy. It is a continuous process and we should never think that we have achieved everything. We will always be learning and experiencing as we walk with the Lord. The Bible tells us that the Holy Spirit is able to teach us all things and will remind us of everything (John 14:26). The Holy Spirit is in us; therefore we can do great things in God and speak His Word to others that will transform lives. Be brave, be tactful and be wise as we speak prophetic words.

As we all have a prophetic role to play, let us endeavour to speak positive words to ourselves and to others daily. The following are some words that we can declare over ourselves and others. These words are able to encourage, strengthen and comfort us on our journey.

- I am created to rule and have dominion.
- I am light and salt in this world.
- I am growing and becoming stronger in Christ.
- All negative thoughts are under my feet.
- Our Lord is able to rescue us from the hands of our enemies.
- We are more than a conqueror.
- Jesus will never leave us. We are His children.
- Anything or anyone assigned to discourage, hurt, or hinder us, I command to be removed in the great name of Jesus.
- With His anointing, all yokes are broken off my life.
- God is my present help in times of trouble.
- The Lord has given us endurance, strength, unity, hope and eternal life through the resurrection.
- No weapon formed against us will prosper.
- We are blessed with all spiritual blessings in heavenly places.
- I am strong and courageous.
- Our family is blessed, our community is blessed and our churches are blessed.
- I am protected by angels.
- We will use all our skills, talents and abilities the Lord has invested in us.
- Our generation will put away the deeds of darkness and put on the armour of light.
- I will live together with Christ, and will remain true to the faith.
- I am in the inheritance that can never perish.
- I am the apple of God's eye.

- I am justified by faith.
- I will excel in all areas of my life.
- I am victorious through Christ.
- I am the Lord's servant.
- I am strong in the Lord.
- God has filled me with good things.
- The mighty one has done great things for us.
- His mercy extends to those who fear Him.
- He has helped us His servants.
- We will serve the Lord without fear.

These are some of the words we are to prophesy. You can speak them as well, or choose your own positive words. There are many, many other great prophetic words that you can choose to say and as you say them your life and the situations around you will be transformed.

The Lord has not changed. His Words are still powerful and are able to change any issue we may encounter. So let's continue to speak prophetic words and strengthen ourselves and others. We are also told to encourage each other daily.

> *But encourage one another daily, as long as it is called today, so that none of you may be hardened by sin's deceitfulness* (Hebrews 3:13).

Let us take positive words and surround ourselves and others daily. As we study His Word, we will be able to bring changes to ourselves and others. As the scripture reminds us: *But everyone who prophesies speaks to men for their strengthening, encouragement and comfort. He who speaks in tongues edifies himself but he who prophesies edifies the church. I would like every one of you to speak in tongues, but I would rather have you prophesy. (*1 Corinthians 14:3-5 NIV)

Life and death are in your tongue, so let's speak life.

PROPHESY OVER OUR NATIONS

As we prophesy to others and ourselves, let us also take time to prophesy to our nations. Wherever you live on this earth, you are to speak prophetic words over your country, just as others did. Elisha, Jeremiah, Isaiah, Joel and others used words to raise the dead, healed sicknesses, eradicated poverty and spoke to people in authority. Therefore, we can do the same to our nations. We have got The Word and the Holy Spirit to do the same. Jesus also spoke and brought changes and we are His followers. The scripture tells us: *You dear children are from God and have overcome them, because the one who is in you is greater than the one who is in the world* (1 John 4:4).

There is an excellent example in the scripture of prophetic utterance that changed the economic situation of an entire nation. If we look carefully at chapters 6 and 7 of 2 Kings we will see how Elisha spoke to a situation in Samaria and changed the economic situation for the whole country. The nation of Samaria was experiencing famine after they were invaded; the people were even eating each other's children. But Elisha spoke in the midst of the famine and told the people that there would be abundance shortly and, just as he said, the exact thing happened. (See Chapter 7) None of us should be negative whenever we are faced with difficulties; we are to speak blessings, positive words always. The scripture tells us that: *Whatever you decide to do will be accomplished and light will shine on the road ahead of you* (Job 22:28). So whatever we decide to change with our words can be changed. Our attitude should be the same as that of Christ Jesus (Philippians 2:5).

The scripture shows us that negative words give a negative outcome and positive words give a positive outcome (2 Kings:7) so let's speak these positive words over our nations:

- The Lord is doing amazing things amongst us.
- Favour, peace and compassion are overtaking my country.
- We will live in harmony with each other.
- Our children, neighbours, family and friends have the power to gain wealth.

- We will strive to love our neighbours as ourselves.
- Our leaders will rule well with wisdom and compassion.
- Crime and violence are disappearing from our land.
- Poverty, destitution, and hatred are in the past.
- Our nation will feed on your Word.
- Our land is fruitful.
- New jobs and resources are available to all.
- Our leaders will depend on the Lord for protection, wisdom and favour.
- God has filled the nation with good things.
- Our nation will turn to God.
- God's Word will be preached, in season and out of season.
- We will say no to ungodliness and worldly passion and live upright and godly lives.
- Our nations will avoid every kind of evil.

God has already delegated authority to us, so we are able to bless whatever we choose to.

OBSTACLES WE MAY FACE AS WE PROPHESY

There are times when we may face obstacles as we prophesy. None of us is exempt from uncertainties, disappointments and grief in this world. There are times when people may not want to listen to us as we speak to them. There are also times the situations that we prophesy to may appear to be very difficult and we may even feel defeated. But we are to take courage and prophesy in spite of all the obstacles. Jesus will never let any of us down. He calls us to prophesy and He will never leave us or forsake us. Some of the Old Testament prophets were beaten, thrown in a cistern and rejected. The prophet Amos was rejected and called a traitor. (See Amos 7:10-12) But they all spoke out against injustice and we can read about their work today.

The apostle Paul experienced rejection when he warned the crew of danger and turmoil. He told them of the danger but they listened to the pilot instead of Paul. It reads:

Much time had been lost, and sailing had already become dangerous because by now it was after the Fast. So Paul warned them, "Men, I can see that our voyage is going to be disastrous and bring great loss to the ship and cargo, and to our own lives also." But the centurion, instead of listening to what Paul said, followed the advice of the pilot and of the owner of the ship.

(Acts 27:9-11)

Many times we may erect our own barriers and prevent our prophecy from being effective. Some excuses we use are:

'I cannot do it.'

'People won't listen to me.'

'I am not good enough.'

'I cannot speak properly.'

And many other negative declarations. It is important that we all take positive steps and speak prophetic words.

PERSONAL EXPERIENCES

Over the years, I have had believers prophesy to me and their words encouraged and strengthened me. I can also say from my own experiences that prophecy is very, very real and empowering, and it is still appropriate in our world today. Some of the believers who prophesied to me were pastors and other of my church brothers and sisters. They have spoken positive words to me that were dynamic and amazing. The times when they have spoken and comforted me, I was broken, discouraged and felt that my life had no meaning. But God loves us and He knows when to send others to speak positive words to us. For example, one Sunday morning I was in church feeling very discouraged. I did not have a job or a place of my own and I honestly did not feel like serving the Lord. But that same morning, my pastor, Pastor Calvin Young, came over to me and prophesied over me. He did not know anything about my circumstances. Yet, he encouraged me by speaking words to me that lifted me out of the low and hopeless state I was in. They were powerful words because the words were a true reflection of my situation.

I can fully remember him saying these words: "Jasmine, all I can see over you is God's favour and blessings."

AND BOY, DID I NEED TO HEAR THOSE WORDS!

The Lord used him to speak those positive words that brought hope. I was surprised to know that the Lord sent someone to speak to me and to encourage me, when I was at my low state. I left the service feeling much, much better that day, even though my circumstances did not change immediately. That prophecy lifted me and I felt a greater and deeper desire to serve the Lord. Our God is real!

Some of my church sisters have also spoken in my life when I was feeling low and depressed. I can remember one Sunday morning, I was feeling so discouraged when one of my church sisters, Mavis Parnell, turned to me and prophesied. She said: "Jasmine, the Lord says you are to wait on Him. It's His time, and everything will happen in His time." Those words were so powerful and uplifting, they encouraged my heart.

I can also remember other church sisters who prophesied over my life on two different occasions. One of them was Carol Campbell and the other was Jackie Williams. Carol Campbell encouraged me, with these words, "God has not forgotten you. You just have to wait on Him." I was struggling financially and I was also in debt. Then Jackie Williams came over to me and said, "The Lord is going to restore all that the devil has stolen." Those words that these sisters prophesied to me were so uplifting, I can never forget those words or those moments.

All of these individuals have helped to change my life by the powerful prophetic words that they have spoken to me. Each prophetic word brought hope to me. It wasn't long after they had spoken into my life that the Lord visited me early one morning and told me to start writing. The Lord has fulfilled his words by restoring my confidence.

On some occasions the Lord has used me to prophesy into other people's lives. Many of these individuals have come back to me and said, "You have spoken words in my life and encouraged me and you have also spoken to situations I was going through which I did not tell you about." None of us knows when the Lord will download specific words to us to prophesy to others He can use any of us, His followers, to speak at crucial moments. We are to listen to His voice and be obedient.

None of us should doubt the power of God. He knows all things and He knows all about us. His Spirit is in us and will teach us all things and remind us of everything (John 14:25).

> *We have not received the Spirit of the world but the Spirit who is from God, that we may understand what God has freely given us. This is what we speak, not in words thought by human wisdom but in words thought by the Spirit, expressing spiritual truths in spiritual words.*

(1 Corinthians 2:12-13)

FALSE PROPHETS

As we read about the power and benefits that prophetic words can bring to our lives, we should also be aware that there are false prophets in our world. The scripture warns us of false prophets, people who will deceive many (Matthew 24:11). The scripture states:

> *Watch out for false prophets. They come to you in sheep clothing, but inwardly they are ferocious wolves. By their fruit you will recognise them. Do people pick grapes from thorn bushes, or figs from thistles? Likewise, every good tree bears good fruit, but a bad tree bears bad fruit. A good tree cannot bear bad fruit, and a bad tree cannot bear good fruit. Every*

tree that does not bear good fruit is cut down and thrown into the fire. Thus by their fruit you will recognise them.

(Matthew 7:15-20 NIV)

But there will be false prophets among the people, just as there will be false teachers among you. They will secretly introduce destructive heresies, even denying the sovereign Lord who brought them, bringing swift destruction on themselves. Many will follow their shameful ways and will bring the way of truth into disrepute. In their greed these will exploit you with stories they have made up.

(2 Peter 2:1-3 NIV)

If people are not in line with God's Word, His instruction and teaching, we should be careful of their actions and not accept or allow them to speak over our lives. If someone is rebellious, disobedient, critical and greedy and has no intention to change, then we should not listen to their word. All activities that are not in accordance with God's Word should be avoided (Acts 13:6). We are to be on the look-out for all false actions. The scripture states that **not** everyone who says to me, 'Lord, Lord', will enter the kingdom of heaven. Many will prophesy in His name and drive out demons and perform many miracles, but they will not enter the Kingdom (Matthew 7:21-23).

There are severe penalties awaiting those who are deceiving others (Revelation 20:10).

If you have deceived anyone in the past and are still deceiving others, please pray this prayer and ask the Lord to forgive you.

DEAR LORD JESUS, PLEASE FORGIVE ME OF ALL MY DECEITS AND DECEPTIONS. PLEASE CHANGE MY HEART AND HELP ME TO LOVE YOU AND BE OBEDIENT TO YOUR WORDS. GIVE ME A NEW DESIRE AS OF TODAY, THANK YOU LORD. AMEN.

You can be changed today by praying this prayer and by changing your action. Our Lord Jesus will forgive you and transform your life, so that you can be the person He wants you to be and speak dynamic words that are effective.

This chapter has mentioned some of the prophetic work of old. It has also shown some of the privileges we have to prophesy in the 21st century. We are aware that we are all empowered by the Holy Spirit, and that we can all speak God's sharp, awesome, transforming Word and bring hope, life and transformation in our world. There are many situations to speak over. There are also barriers, obstacles and false prophets that we may encounter. Nevertheless, we are to continue to prophesy, as we walk this Christian journey, over all: **a**dversities, **b**aggage, **c**riminal actions, **e**vil, **f**ear, **g**un crime, **h**opelessness, **i**njustice, **j**ealousy, **k**illing, **l**oneliness, **m**ountains, **n**egative actions, **o**utrageous actions, **p**overty, **q**uarrelling, **r**eproach, **s**tormy situations, **t**roubles, **u**nforgiveness, **v**iolence, **w**ar, **y**oke, prophesy in **Z**ion and all over the world. Tell the impossible to become possible, in the name of Jesus prophesy! We will be successful.

Chapter Nine

TAKE THE BEST CARE OF YOUR BODY EAT HEALTHILY AND EXERCISE

As we strive to look after our spiritual well-being, it is essential to take care of our physical body as well. We are made up of spirit, soul and body; our Lord cares for the total man. We are to take care of our bodies, by eating the right types of food, exercising and sleeping well.

It is crucial that we have a balanced diet. We can have a balanced diet by eating different types of food and vegetables. Our bodies need different types of nutrients to provide us with energy and build us up. Our bodies mainly need proteins, carbohydrates, fats, vitamins, minerals and water. It is important that we do not fill our bodies with junk food, but eat healthily, so that we will be able to serve the Lord and fulfil our purposes in good health.

The following are the main types of food that we need to eat in order to remain fit and healthy:

VITAMINS AND MINERALS: We obtain vitamins and minerals from fruit, tomatoes, melons, strawberries, fish, milk, eggs, kidneys and leafy vegetables.

CARBOHYDRATES: Carbohydrates are found in bread, sweets, biscuits, pasta, apples, sweet corn, cereals, baked and red kidney beans, lentils, green peppers, and bananas, baked and boiled potatoes.

PROTEINS: Proteins are obtained from both plants and animals. Plant proteins include peas, beans and lentils and seeds. Animal proteins are obtained from poultry, fish, eggs, cheese, butter, milk and yoghurt.

FATS: Fats are found in fish, chicken, vegetable oils, eggs, avocadoes, butter, meat, cream and whole milk.

We should also drink plenty of water and other liquids.

There are some foods that we should not consume too much of. Some are too greasy and some too fattening.

If we cannot cook, we can learn to cook. Nothing is impossible. Some foods are easy to cook, such as potatoes, rice, chicken, vegetables and pasta. These foods are easy to prepare.

EXERCISE: Exercise is necessary to keep us fit and healthy. It helps to reduce anxiety and aids sleep. So we are to take regular exercise. There are various exercises we can do, such as jogging, swimming or going to the gym. It doesn't matter how old or young you are, there is always some exercise that is appropriate for you. Housework, such as cleaning, cooking, ironing and gardening are also good exercise.

SPORT: Many of us enjoy sport and should continue doing our sporting activities. There are many sports that we can be involved in to keep us fit, such as cycling, golf, tennis, football and others.

HOBBIES: Many of us have other activities which we love doing. We are to take time to enjoy the things we like doing, be it dancing, painting, travelling or collecting, to mention just a few. Whatever we enjoy doing, we should not give up on them because of our relationship with Christ.

We should look after our children while they are in our care, making sure they are properly fed, cared for and loved. And we should encourage them to do the things they enjoy doing. We should also to teach them proper hygiene, how to tidy up, wash up and clean their surroundings.

We should also look out for the children in our communities, make sure they are properly cared for. And should you discern anyone in danger or abused please inform the proper authorities. They have the expertise to decide what is best for our children safety.

Furthermore, I realise that children and situations have changed with parents and children nowadays from when we were growing up. However there are still certain principles that must be applied in all generations. All children should be taught manners, should be disciplined in love, should be taught wrong from right and should be fed and washed in all societies and races.

MENTAL HEALTH: Many of us or our family members and friends struggle with our mental issues. It is highly recommended that we protect our mental health. If you are having difficulties with your mental state, here are some tips:

- Keep active.
- Take regular exercise.
- Eat healthily.
- Eat plenty of fruit and vegetables.
- Eat oily fish at least 4 times per week.
- Drink alcohol in moderation.
- Value and respect yourself and others.
- Speak to someone about how you are feeling.
- Keep in touch with your friends and family
- Learn something new, a skill or a language.
- Take a break and relax.
- Don't try to do too much. Ask someone for help if you need it.
- Get involved in something positive and make a contribution.

The above examples can be applied to churches all over the world. In the chapters I have listed, we should all follow these principles and we will be successful in our lives. We aim to take care of ourselves and those for whom we are responsible.

Chapter Ten

CONTINUE TO LEARN AND GROW

Now that you have read this book on ways to live a successful Christian life, I do hope you will not stop here, but continue to read and grow in the Lord and in all other areas of your life. Take some time to reflect on what you have learnt and continue to develop in Christ. The apostle Paul mentioned that we are to build ourselves up by admonishing and teaching, so that we can be perfect in Christ (Colossians 1:28). There is no stagnation in Christ. He wants us to aim to achieve more and more in all we do. We are to aim to grow spiritually, intellectually, socially, and in knowledge. God's Word makes it clear that He wants us to continue to achieve in many ways.

He gives us apostles, prophets, evangelists, pastors and teachers in our churches (Ephesians 4:11-12) so that they can train up others in different ministries, and assist them to move from one stage to the next.

Jesus Himself also obtained continuous wisdom while He was here on earth. The Bible says: A*nd Jesus grew in wisdom and in stature, and in favour with God and men* (Luke 2:52).

He set an example while He was here on Earth by gaining wisdom and He was always teaching and preaching to others so that they could continue to learn. (See Matthew 4:23)

There are many areas where we are to continue to learn, but most importantly we are to continue to learn about:

- Jesus
- God's will for our lives
- Ourselves
- Our career
- And about others

LEARN ABOUT JESUS: As children of Christ, we should aim to expand our knowledge of Him. We are to continue reading His Word and discover more about Him, continue speaking to Him. Let prayer be the focal point on our journey with Christ. Continue to learn how to worship Him. Christ needs our worship. Worship Him in all we do and learn to worship Him better. Continue to serve Him and to tell others about Him. Jesus lives inside of us and He will continue to reveal Himself to us in many ways, through the Holy Spirit. The scripture tells us that the Holy Spirit will bring all things to our remembrance.

There are CDs, books and other Christian literature that we should listen to and read. They will assist us to learn about Jesus. We will also learn about Him by attending church regularly and by attending Bible school.

As we learn about Him, we will find that His power is higher and deeper than us and His ways are beyond what we can ever discover. We will gain wisdom, power and strength as we continue to learn about the King. The Word of God says: *The treasure of wisdom and knowledge is hidden in Christ* (Colossians 2:3).

LEARN ABOUT HIS WILL FOR YOUR LIFE: As we learn about Christ, we will also learn about His will for our lives. There are times when we will have to make decisions about our jobs, choice of partners, ministries and many other matters. During these times, we will have to learn how to seek Him for answers and how to be obedient to His voice. Before we came to know the Lord we did things to please ourselves, we did things without praying or asking any questions. Now that we are His followers, it is imperative that we seek Him in all our ways. We have been bought by the Lord (1 Corinthians 6:19-20).

And as we follow Him, we are obedient to His will. Whenever we are faced with a decision we should continue to turn to Him and seek Him for direction. God is always willing to show us His good pleasure and perfect will (Romans 12:2b).

LEARN ABOUT YOURSELF: As we learn and develop in other areas, we should also learn more about ourselves. We can learn to forgive, to be more tolerant, understanding and caring. We can learn how to get on with people, to be better listeners, how to give, share and to show respect.

The only way we can be properly equipped and function efficiently in this changing world is to continue learning more about ourselves and aim to adjust. We should also aim to learn new skills, learn about things that interest us, learn **not** to be too quick to judge and condemn, but to forgive and to assist in whatever way we can.

LEARN MORE ABOUT YOUR CAREER: Whatever sector you work in, it is important that you continue to learn and develop in your career. Always aim to climb to the next level in your profession. There are many ways we can learn and develop ourselves and there are many learning tools that we can obtain information from. Society is always changing, and we all need to gain more knowledge.

Some of you will be called into full-time ministry, which will lay great demands on you to read widely. You will need to continue to learn and grow.

CONTINUE TO LEARN ABOUT OTHERS: It is wise to continue to learn about others. We are all different people, from different countries and cultures, with different upbringings, religious beliefs, values and skills. We are to continue learning about others and how to love and appreciate each other. And to keep praying and speaking positive words to others.

TOOLS WE CAN USE TO ENHANCE OUR LEARNING: There are many tools that are available to enhance our learning, which include:

BOOKS AND MAGAZINES: There are many books and magazines available to provide information. We should continue to read and increase our knowledge. Read books especially in areas which particularly interest you.

THE MEDIA: The media is a very important source of information. It is not wise to withdraw ourselves from all these sources. We are to listen to the radio, watch television and read the newspapers. I am not recommending all the programmes on the television or radio, but there are some informative programmes we should watch or listen to so that we can be informed. We should also continue to listen to CDs, DVDs and podcasts. *Knowledge is better than choice gold* (Proverbs 8:10).

WORDS: Our words are powerful tools and as we learn new words, these will help us to develop our confidence and understanding. It is essential that we continue to speak positive words, to ourselves and to others. For example, always tell yourself that you are blessed, you are an over-comer, you are free from condemnation and you are complete in Christ. Continue to say these positive words.

OBSERVING AND MENTORSHIP: We can also learn from others. Learn about what they did to be successful. Learn about the obstacles they had to go through to get to where they are. As we learn we will also realise that some have failed many times before they achieved anything. We can also learn how to avoid making some of the mistakes others have made.

SEMINARS: Seminars and conferences are important events that we are to make an effort to attend. Many churches and other institutions organise conferences and seminars each year. As we attend these events, we gather ideas and learn many new things. We will learn a lot about the Christian walk; as we listen to other Christian teachings and encouragement, our lives will be challenged.

TRAINING: Many of us can attend colleges and universities and we should not think that we are too young or too old to learn. We can all learn something new, whatever age we are. There are many courses on offer in our colleges and universities. As we continue to learn and gain knowledge, we will have a better sense of purpose and be more productive.

THE INTERNET: We can learn and increase our knowledge of many subjects by obtaining information from the internet. The internet has all kinds of information that we can tap into. We can all obtain information that will increase our knowledge. We can use all these resources and develop ourselves. Always be on the look-out for new ways to develop.

ALWAYS ENCOURAGE YOUNG PEOPLE: It is important that we continue to encourage our young people to learn and develop. If you are a young person, be an example for other young people. Paul, writing to Timothy, encouraged him on so many matters. Paul wrote strong positive words to Timothy to strengthen and empower him, for example: *Flee the evil desires of youth, and pursue righteousness, faith, love and peace, along with those who call on the Lord out of pure heart* (1 Timothy 2:22 NIV).

As adults we are to encourage young people to learn and continue learning. The Bible says: *We are to seek Him first and his righteousness and all things will be given to us* (Matthew 6:33). We should encourage them to give God first place in their lives and to develop their abilities and talents. It is essential that they know from an early age that studying is not boring, unexciting or irrelevant, but is rewarding. Remind them of the future. Young people are the future generation and they should be knowledgeable.

Many of them will become leaders of the future, so we are to aim to build their self-confidence and self-esteem. We should not criticize or speak disrespectfully to any of them, but allow them to pursue the field that they are interested in. Some may not be interested in academic study at university level, but they may have other skills and potential. Some may be interested in sports, in music or other skills; always encourage them to be the best.

THE BENEFITS OF KNOWLEDGE: We can all receive some benefit from learning. Learning helps us to:

- maximise our potential
- gain understanding
- build our confidence
- empower and make us proud
- enhance our promotion prospects
- create excitement and a sense of achievement

None of us should give up on learning. As we learn new skills, we will be inspired. The Bible says that the fear of the Lord is the beginning of knowledge (Proverbs 1:7). We all have to continue learning. None of us knows it all; only God.

It is not always easy to start learning something new. At times there are obstacles to prevent us from learning as we venture out. It can have implications for our private and family lives, our work, and it can also be stretching at times. But we all have to make an effort and be determined. We should organise ourselves, seek support and tell ourselves that it's not too late.

The Lord promises many things in this life: to protect us, to supply our needs, to keep us in perfect peace, to answer us when we call on Him. However, we have to do our part to be successful. We have to continue to pray, speak and learn. We cannot stop after we have achieved certain benefits. Be prepared to work, to learn and to do things that will change your life.

God promised that He will do a new thing in our lives, look out for new developments. *"See, I am doing a new thing! Now it springs up; do you not perceive it? I am making a way in the desert and streams in wasteland"* (Isaiah 43:19).

There are many knowledgeable and skilful people that we can read about in the Bible. For example, Moses wrote the first five books of the Old Testament. Paul wrote most of the New Testament. Other writers are Matthew, Mark, Luke, John, Peter and many others (Colossians 4:14). Peter was a fisherman. And Paul was a tent-maker; they all had skills and talents. Learning and acquiring new skills is important for all of us. We should all follow these examples and acquire knowledge and skills.

Take the initiative and start to do something today. Some started young; some later in life. It doesn't matter how or where you start; the whole idea is to start and continue learning and grow.

Nothing remains unchanged; there are always changes. Our situations change: we might change our jobs, our ministry, our family circumstances and our mentality. So it is important to learn and grow in Christ.

Over the years I have read many books, the Bible, books on animals, history, leadership, management, science, Christian literature and more. I am glad that I was always reading. I did not know that the Lord was preparing me to write. Now that I am writing I can refer back to those books, look on other authors' writing and be a better writer. I am now benefiting from all those years I invested in reading. As we learn, we will become more focused, have a better sense of purpose, and be more effective.

Continue to read this book and other materials and learn more. I release the blessings of God on all those who have read this book. I hope that God's favour will surround you, His love, peace, joy, prosperity, good health, humility, wisdom, victory, provision, and the grace of God will continue to be with you as you learn about Him and grow to live a productive and SUCCESSFUL CHRISTIAN LIFE.

Continue to learn about: His blessings, learn about caring, learn about devotion, learn about evangelism, learn about faithfulness, learn about giving, learn about healing, learn about impurity, learn about justice, learn about kindness, learn about love, learn about meekness, learn about other nations, learn about overcoming weakness, learn about **p**eace, learn good **q**ualities, learn about **r**eligions, learn about **s**cience**,** learn about **t**echnology, learn about **u**nselfishness, learn about **v**isions, learn about **w**itnessing, learn about **y**ourself and learn about **Z**ion.

KEEP LEARNING!

The path to living a victorious life is not always easy, but if we continue to be obedient and follow God's directions, we will be able to live a successful Christian life. Based on my personal experiences of serving the Lord for over thirty years and other people's experiences, these are some of the main principles that I have practised.

The book outlines the importance of reading God's Word, praying, giving, telling others about Jesus and showing us how to exercise our faith in God. I have outlined the ways to say 'no' consistently to sin so that we can learn how to serve others in the Lord's house, including learning how to prophesy to each other and also how to take the best care of ourselves. The final chapter states that we are to continue learning and developing ourselves and be all that God has ordained us to be. I hope that you will continue to read this book and put all its principles into practice. These steps are what we all need to live a dynamic and successful Christian life in the twenty-first century.

Jesus loves us and He wants us to follow Him and to be the best. He also promised us all His blessings. If you are contemplating giving up on this Christian walk, please ask Him to strengthen you and to open your eyes to see all the good things that He has in store for you. The Lord Jesus is willing and waiting to bless us abundantly and I just want to leave the following blessings with you:

If you fully obey the Lord your God and carefully follow all His commandments that I have given you today, the Lord your God will set you high above all the nations on Earth. All these blessings will come upon you and accompany you if you obey the Lord your God.

You will be blessed in the city and blessed in the country.

The fruit of your womb will be blessed and the crops of your land and the young of your livestock, the calves of your herds and the lambs of your flocks.

Your basket and your kneading dough will be blessed.

You will be blessed when you come in and blessed when you go out.

The Lord will grant that the enemies who rise up against you will be defeated before you. They will come at you from one direction but flee from you in seven.

The Lord will send a blessing on your barns and on everything you put your hands to. The Lord your God will bless you in the land he is giving you. The Lord will establish you as his holy people, as he promised on oath, if you keep the commands of the Lord your God and walk in his ways. Then all the people on Earth will see that you are called by the name of the Lord, and they will fear you.

The Lord will grant you abundant prosperity in the fruit of your womb, the young of your livestock and the crop of your ground in the land he swore to your forefathers to give you. The Lord will open the heavens, the storehouse of his bounty, to send rain on your land in seasons and to bless all the work of your hand. You will lend to many nations but will borrow from none. The Lord will make you the head, not the tail. If you pay attention to the commands of the Lord your God that I give you this day and carefully follow them, you will always be at the top, never at the bottom. Do not turn aside from any of the commands I give you today, to the right or to the left, follow other Gods and serving them (Deuteronomy 28:1-14 NIV).

I hope you have been blessed and strengthened. Please let me know by e-mailing me at:

Jasmine@hotmail.co.uk

Lightning Source UK Ltd.
Milton Keynes UK
UKOW040656041212

203134UK00004B/248/P